SPIRIT CALLING

~ ~ as whispered to 'The Listener' ~ Jane Apter

Copyright © 2013 by Jane Apter

Spirit Calling
by Jane Apter

Printed in the United States of America

ISBN 9781626970595

All rights reserved solely by the author. The author guarantees all contents are original and do not infringe upon the legal rights of any other person or work. No part of this book may be reproduced in any form without the permission of the author. The views expressed in this book are not necessarily those of the publisher.

Unless otherwise indicated, Bible quotations are taken from The New International Version (NIV) of The Holy Bible. Copyright © 1973, 1978, 1984 by Biblica, Inc.®. Also used are the following versions, according to http://www.biblegateway.com/; The Amplified Bible (AMP). Copyright © 1954, 1958, 1962, 1964, 1965, 1987 by The Lockman Foundation NAS; The Easy-to-Read Version (ERV). Copyright © 2006 by World Bible Translation Center; The Holy Bible, English Standard Version (ESV). Copyright © 2001 by Crossway Bibles, a division of Good News Publishers; The Good News Translation (GNT). Copyright © 1992 by American Bible Society; The King James Version (KJV); The Message (MSG). Copyright © 1993, 1994, 1995, 1996, 2000, 2001, 2002 by Eugene H. Peterson; The New American Standard Bible (NASB). Copyright © 1960, 1962, 1963, 1968, 1971, 1972, 1973, 1975, 1977, 1995 by The Lockman Foundation; The Holy Bible, New

Century Version® (NCV). Copyright © 2005 by Thomas Nelson, Inc; The New English Translation (NET) NET Bible.® Copyright © 1996-2006 by Biblical Studies Press, L.L.C. http://netbible.com; The New International Reader's Version (NIRV). Copyright © 1996, 1998 by Biblica; The Holy Bible, New King James Version. Copyright © 1982 by Thomas Nelson, Inc; The Holy Bible, New Living Translation (NLT). Copyright © 1996, 2004, 2007 by Tyndale House Foundation; The J. B. Phillips, (PHILLIPS) "The New Testament in Modern English". Copyright © 1962 by HarperCollins; and The Worldwide English (New Testament) (WE). Copyright © 1969, 1971, 1996, 1998 by SOON Educational Publications.

www.xulonpress.com

[INTRODUCTION]

The LORD has declared this day that you are His treasured possession.
[DEUTERONOMY 26:18a]

"You are Mine, child. You are Mine to hold — to hold very still — until all your fears are washed away. You are Mine — You are My treasured possession. Go in Peace. . . . Go in My Strength. . . . Child, you are Mine. That is what gives you worth."

GOD CALLING was my most precious devotional book in college many years ago. It was put away in book boxes through many moves. In 2000, I got Encephalitis — a brain infection that debilitated my memory and cognitive thinking skills. One aftereffect of that illness was Peripheral Neuropathy, which caused my fingers, hands, feet, toes to be numb and stiff. All of this put me at the complete mercy of the LORD, Who became my sole source of everything. I was totally dependent on Him for every movement, every thought, every decision — everything. It drew me into a deep, intimate, precious relationship with my Savior, Father, Nurturer, Provider, Protector, Shepherd, Deliverer, Redeemer, Friend. And through that time, once again, GOD CALLING became my most precious source of intimacy with Him. As I recorded my thoughts & prayers in the journal space in that precious book, Words would pour out of my pen that I knew were not mine. They were His Precious Words whispered to my heart. At first it was very occasional that I would hear those Words, but then, it became an almost daily occurrence. It became clear to my heart that I really was to compile all those Precious Words that His Powerful yet Gentle Spirit had been calling to my heart . . . and now to yours. . . . .

[FORWARD]

I will listen to what God the LORD will say.
[PSALM 85:8a]

*((Dear LORD, Your WORDS are
most precious to me.
I treasure them.
No one else can touch my heart like You, O
LORD!
I so want to be a channel of Your Love!))*

"You touch My Heart, too, child. It is very dear to My Heart to have you here in My Arms. Relax in My Arms. Feel My Presence. This is only the beginning, My daughter. I have set you apart for Me. I share My WORDS with you — to be a comfort to the lonely, the broken-hearted, the hurting — to speak to, and be a source of Life for the lost, for those desiring deeper intimacy with Me. Your pen is flowing with My Grace, My Love, My Peace. Just wait before Me. . . .Be open. . . .Be humble. . . .Be still. . . .Be Mine. Then, you shall hear My Whispers to your softened heart.

— *You shall hear My Spirit Calling.*"

*Write down the revelation and
make it plain on tablets
so that a herald may run with it.*
[HABAKKUK 2:2]

SPIRIT CALLING

Jan. 1

He performs wonders that cannot be fathomed,
miracles that cannot be counted.
[JOB 5:9; 9:10]

"I am drawing My people back to Me by the outpouring of My Spirit upon the earth. Be a channel of My Spirit. Touch the wounded with My Healing, My Restoring Power. Listen for My Call. Listen for My Voice — not the voice of the multitude. Listen for My Still Small — yet Powerful — Voice. I whisper the Secrets of Life, Love, Freedom, to the trembling heart — to the searching ear — the searching soul — the broken heart. Be a vessel of My Calming Spirit — My Gentle Love — My Tender Mercy — My Calming Peace — My Nurturing Spirit. Claim My Power. Move only at the prompting of My Spirit. Stand firm against the enemy's voice. Be open and willing to hear My Spirit calling, and you will see wonders yet unseen."

October 2
Jan. 2

When Your WORDS came, I ate them; they were my joy and my heart's delight.
[JEREMIAH 15:16a]

"Make My WORDS your delight. — Not only the WORDS written down for you from centuries ago, but the WORDS you hear spoken to your heart — to your innermost being — as you sit quietly before Me. But even more than that, remember, I am the WORD made flesh to dwell among you. Be fed by My very Presence here with you. Make Me your heart's delight."

Jan. 3

You are priceless to Me. I love you and honor you.
[ISAIAH 43:4a (NIRV)]

"Life with Me — intimacy with Me — truly is a Love Story. You are My beloved and I want intimate communion with you. You are My precious creation. I created you as an image of My Love. Never doubt your worth in My Eyes. Failures and faults — covered with the Blood of the Lamb — have no power to damage your worth in My Eyes. If it were not so, no one could stand in My Presence. No one is worthy to behold My Glory, unless they are clothed in My Robe of Righteousness and covered by the Blood of the Lamb. In My Presence, you reflect My Glory. In My Presence, My Love is made manifest. Come into My Presence in intimate communion with Me. Intimacy with Me — life with Me — truly is a Love Story."

Jan. 4

The Lord longs to be gracious to you.
He rises to show you compassion.
[ISAIAH 30:18a]

"When failure and strife is all you feel — all you see — look deep into My Eyes. See there My Love, My Compassion, My yearning to comfort you and support you — and yet, to correct you, by pruning away the lifelessness, the fruitless unhealthy weak parts of you, to bring forth newness of life — that you may bear much fruit for My Kingdom."

Jan. 5

We are the clay, You are the Potter;
we are all the work of Your Hand.
[ISAIAH 64:8b]

"Though it is humbling, yielding to Me in total surrender produces a moldable vessel. As you continue that surrender — yielding to My every move — I bring forth a priceless vessel that I can then fill with My Mercy and Grace, My Love and Peace — to be poured out on those around you."

Jan. 6

The LORD gives strength to His people;
The LORD blesses His people with Peace.
[PSALM 29:11]

"No matter what is going on in the world around you, you can be at peace if you hold tight to My Hand and follow My lead. No power can come against you when you are within My Inner Court — My Holy of Holies. Commune with Me. — In My Presence there is Perfect Peace . . . Rest for your weary soul . . . Strength for your trembling heart. Sit quietly in My Presence. Then go forth in My Peace."

Jan. 7

I guide you in the way of wisdom and lead you along straight paths.
[PROVERBS 4:11]

"Never fear! I am always here beside you, to lead and guide you along life's pathways. You are important to Me. I created you for My pleasure, and for a specific purpose in My Kingdom. Walk very close to Me and I will direct your paths."

Jan. 8

Keep me as the apple of Your Eye;
Hide me in the shadow of Your Wings.
[PSALM 17:8]

"In your weariness, I am your Strength. In your loneliness, I am your Constant Companion. In your sadness ~~ in your fear ~~ I am He Who gathers you into My Arms and carries you close to My Heart. In your suffering, I am your Suffering Savior. In your times of emotional despair and feelings of worthlessness, I am your Stronghold, your Loving Abba Father, Who says to you, 'Precious child, you are My treasured possession, the apple of My Eye.'"

Jan. 9

From heaven He made you hear His Voice to discipline you.
[DEUTERONOMY 4:36a]

"I speak to you not only to instruct you and comfort you, but also to bring you into obedience, through the washing of My WORD. This must be a daily practice. — Each day you need the washing of My WORD to make you whole. You need My full embrace, to walk fully in My Will. Let My WORD — Let Me — Let My Presence — embrace you."

Jan. 10

How precious to me are Your Thoughts, O God!

[PSALM 139:17a]

"How precious to Me are your thoughts, child, when they are fixed on Me. Precious indeed are the thoughts of My children when those thoughts are centered on finding My Will, and on seeking My Truths in My WORD that speak directly to your heart. Fix your thoughts on Me, and bring Joy to My Heart, in so doing."

Jan. 11

*So do not fear, for I am with you; do not be
dismayed, for I am your God.
I will strengthen you and help you; I will
uphold you with My Righteous Right Hand.*
[ISAIAH 41:10]

"Do not let your own feelings — or those of others toward
you — alter your course, or stifle your availability to Me.
Do not gauge the impact of your touch, by the emotional
response — or lack thereof — of those around you.
Follow My Lead, and I will set in motion the Works of
My Spirit, which I am using you to administer to others.
What you see on the outside may not at all be what I am
really touching, and moving and shaking, and setting
right by your touch. Be humble, though. Take no pride
in My using you. Pride stifles the impact of My Works.
But fear not, child, I make all things new. Go into this day
that I have given to you, with My Power, My Love, My
Forgiveness, My Strength. . . . So go."

Jan. 12

There is now no condemnation for those who are in Christ Jesus.

[ROMANS 8:1]

"There is now no condemnation in My Heart for you. You are washed by the Blood of the Spotless Lamb. Nothing can change that. You are Mine. My Banner of Love is over you. Against it no power can stand. Be humble. Be strong. Be Mine."

Jan. 13

I have heard your prayer and seen your tears; I will heal you.
[2 KINGS 20:5]

"My people are in need of healing — physical healing, as well as inner healing of their hearts, of their thoughts, of their emotions, their past. What is your healing need today? Think carefully. Is it really what you have perceived it to be? Seek My Peace first and foremost. I have promised in My WORD that I will heal you. In due time, I will heal you. In My Infinite Wisdom, I will heal you. I will work all things together for your good. But please know, that goodness may not be in the form you have desired. Lean on Me. Lean on My Understanding. Lean on Me for Strength and Love and Compassionate Loving-Kindness. Lean on Me — and in that leaning, bow down in worship and praise. Praise wings your cries for help to My Listening Ear, and opens the gates of heaven — releasing My Power over you, to bring that goodness — that healing — into being."

Jan. 14

The LORD longs to be gracious to you;
He rises to show you compassion.
For the LORD is a God of Justice.
Blessed are all who wait for Him.
[ISAIAH 30:18]

"Be calm. Wait. I will open the door for you in due time. Watch and be patient. Go ahead of Me, and you lose your blessings I have in store for you. Watch and wait. You will not be disappointed if you lay it all down, and trust Me — fully trust Me. Wait, and watch. Be at peace. Trust, and you will see My Hand working all things for your good because you love Me, and look to Me for your supply. So, wait."

Jan. 15

*Surely God is my salvation; I will trust
and not be afraid.
The LORD, the LORD, is my strength and my
song; He has become my salvation.*
[ISAIAH 12:2]

"Yes, child, I AM your salvation — your salvation from your fears, your failures, your **self**. . . . Your **self**. . . . It all comes down to **self** — putting **self** on the throne, making **self** all important, making **self** lord of your life — of your innermost being. Take **self** off the throne, and make Me LORD and King of your heart. Only then will I be your strength, your song, your salvation. You choose. . . . Choose Me — and choose Life."

Jan. 16

The tongue that brings healing is a tree of life.
Whoever is kind to the needy honors God.
[PROVERBS 15:14; 14:3]

"Helping another in need feeds your own soul, and fills your heart with Joy. Watch and be ready — at a moment's notice — to fulfill a need of your brother, especially, and of those you have never even met before. A kind word may be all they need, or a small gesture of kindness, or just a listening ear. Be available to be used for their need, and for My Glory. You can be an agent of change — in someone's day, in someone's heart, in someone's life."

Jan. 17

He rewards those who earnestly seek Him.
[HEBREWS 11:6b]

"My Rewards are Kingdom Rewards — Love, Joy, Peace
. . . a wealth of Kingdom friends . . . a vast Kingdom
family to support and love you. . . . And the Richest
Rewards of all — — My Presence . . . coming freely
into My Holy of Holies . . . being covered over with My
Protective Banner of Love . . . My WORDS spoken to
your listening ears — your tender, seeking heart. . . .
Come. . . . Earnestly seek Me. . . . Be Richly rewarded."

Jan. 18

"For I know the plans I have for you,"
declares the LORD.
"Call upon Me and come and pray to Me."
"You will seek Me and find Me when you seek
Me with all your heart."
[JEREMIAH 29:11a,12a,13]

"I have a purpose and a plan for you that you know not yet of. Stay huddled in the Secret Place of My Presence. Abide, and it shall be disclosed to you. Be not in a rush to press on into the future. Many pieces must be set in place for all to be worked together for your good — and the good of those whose lives are also touched. But do seek My Face, My Will for you, each day — each moment. Come running to My Arms and let Me whisper the next step to you — the next phase of the Purpose for your life with Me. Be eager; be zealous; be ready to heed My call."

Jan. 19

*Follow the way of Love and eagerly desire spiritual gifts.
Try to excel in gifts that build up the church.*
[1 CORINTHIANS 14:1a,12b]

"When your days' schedules are altered, look at how I have used you in those moments. Have your spiritual gifts been at work? Have you touched someone's life with My Love? Have you lifted someone's spirits? Have you provided for the needs of one of My own? Is someone else's burden lighter now? Have you reinforced someone's acts of kindness? Have you 'washed someone's feet'?

. . . If so, not a moment's time was wasted. Being a channel of My Love . . . My Life . . . My Touch . . . is one of the dearest works of My Kingdom. Be faithful to My Nudge. Then look back over the beauty along your pathway, seeing all the lives — all the hearts — that you have touched with My Love. Keep a humble heart, and watch My Hand at work in your life."

Jan. 20

I have loved you with an everlasting Love;
I have drawn you with Loving-Kindness.
[JEREMIAH 31:3]

Come to Me, all you who are weary and
burdened, and I will give you rest.
[MATTHEW 11:28]

"When you are weary, I open My Arms to carry you. Too often, you drag yourself from activity to activity, without thought of Me. Child, I want to draw you into My Loving Arms. Do not ignore — do not reject — the Arms of Love stretched out to you. Come, child, come unto Me. I will give you rest — rest amongst the scurry of your day. It only takes a moment, to be drawn into My Arms of Love. That moment of refreshing can make all the difference in your day. . . .Come to Me. I will give you rest."

Jan. 21

Therefore, as we have opportunity, let us do good to all people, especially to those who belong to the family of believers.
[GALATIANS 6:10]

"Treasure the spiritual gifts I have given you. Consider the works that you can do for My Kingdom — for My people — for the hurting, the wounded, the broken ones I bring into your life — into your path, daily. Be ever-watchful for opportunity to be used by Me. — — Not on your own power do you do good works — — but by My Bountiful Gifts of My Strong Power — My Tender Mercy — My Comfort and Compassion — My Generosity. Be My Hands, My Feet, My Touch. And be filled with the Fullness of Joy in so doing."

Jan. 22

You will fill me with Joy in Your Presence,
with eternal pleasures at Your Right Hand.
[PSALM 16:11b]

The LORD your God is with you.
He will quiet you with His Love.
[ZEPHANIAH 3:17]

"Come. Sit at My Feet. Rest your weary head. . . .Lost in My Presence, time stands still, because in My Presence, you are in My Eternal Realm, where time does not exist. Come in silence — fully focused on Me alone. Let My Peace rest your weary heart. Let My Presence fill your emptiness. Let My Presence permeate your innermost being. Let My Presence bring Freedom and Joy to your heart — praise to your lips. Let My Presence quiet your fears. Let My Presence calm your unrest. Let My Presence quiet you with My Love . . . with My Embrace."

Jan. 23

Now devote your heart and soul to seeking the LORD your God.
[1 CHRONICLES 22:19]

"I see your heart. Does it long after Me, even when your flesh cannot — or does not — act on it? When you long for Me with all your heart, you are beautiful to Me — My Pure and Spotless Bride. In the fleeting moments of silence in your day — in the fleeting moments of silence in your spirit — I see the ache, the yearning, to be in My Arms — held securely, and listening to My Voice, soaking up My Mercy, My Love, My Peace, My Joy — whatever your spirit needs that very moment — what your spirit is pouring out to Me. To hear your plea . . . your praise . . . your love — each time your spirit turns to Me — it touches My Heart, and Compassion flows forth from Me to you. Seek Me and know Me more deeply when you seek Me with all your heart . . . when you seek Me, to hear My Whispers . . . when you seek Me, to just be near Me."

Jan. 24

And do not forget to do good
and to share with others.
Obey your leaders and submit to their
authority.
They keep watch over you as men
who must give account.
Obey them so that their work will be a joy,
not a burden,
for that would be of no advantage to you.
[HEBREWS 13:16a,17]

"Submit to those in authority over you. This is not a suggestion — but a command — a command with a promise. Those who sow in peace shall reap a harvest of peace — especially in My Kingdom — in relationships nurtured and anointed by Me."

Jan. 25

*In love He has predestined us to be adopted
as His sons through Jesus Christ,
in accordance with His Pleasure and Will.*
[EPHESIANS 1:5]

*Those who are led by the Spirit of God
are sons of God.
You received the Spirit of sonship. And by
Him we cry, "Abba, Father."*
[ROMANS 8:14,15b]

"When you gave your life over to Me, you received the Spirit of Sonship. That is why I have always called you, 'child.' Your Abba Father — Daddy — is always here for you. Run with Me. Follow in My Footsteps. Step into your Inheritance as My child."

Jan. 26

*The sacrifices of God are a broken spirit,
a broken and contrite heart.*
[PSALM 51:17]

"A humble and contrite heart is what I require — no, desire — of you. As a Father, Who disciplines His child, I desire a humble, teachable, moldable heart — a repentant heart — in My children. When pride takes its course, however, sharp discipline may be required at that point. But, if a humble and contrite heart, is then offered out of a desire to be obedient and totally led by Me, that greatly pleases Me. — That is My desire of you. . . . Self-discipline is much less painful. . . . Which do you choose?"

Jan. 27

Repent, then, and turn to God, so that your sins may be wiped out, that times of refreshing may come from the LORD.
[ACTS 3:19]

"When you turn to Me in repentance and brokenness, you are so precious to Me. When that becomes a natural turning, you see your heart changing from what you formerly were — which you so detested — into what you so desired, but seldom walked out. Let Me wash you from the inside out — changing, melting, remolding your heart into a holy temple of My Spirit, through which My Agape Love, and My Power, freely flow."

Jan. 28

For this reason I remind you to fan into
flame the Gift of God, which is in you
through the laying on of hands.
For God did not give us a spirit of timidity,
but a Spirit of Power.
[2 TIMOTHY 1:6-7]

"All My Power and Authority I give to you, so that you can do all things I call you to do, and so that whatever you bind on earth shall be bound in heaven — and whatever you loose on earth will be loosed in heaven. I give you ALL My Power. Claim it! Use it!! Release it! — Release it over people, over situations, over relationships, over whatever stronghold you discern, whatever evil lurks. Claim it!! Use it!!! — Use it for your protection! — Use it for My Glory. Use it!!!"

Jan. 29

Bear with each other and forgive whatever grievances you may have against one another. Forgive as the LORD forgave you.
[COLOSSIANS 3:13]

"People, words, actions, situations — all these may destroy you, or cause you pain. At those moments, come to My Presence — where Love and open Arms await you. Sweet child, forgive as I have forgiven you. Some of those most hurtful offenses against you, are offenses that have reoccurred over and over. And you say of that person, 'Why don't they see how much it hurts me when they do that?!' — or, 'When will they ever change?!?' Yet, I have forgiven you . . . over and over and over again. Follow My lead. Go and do likewise. The freedom you shall then receive — the release you shall experience — the bondage broken — will set you free from the anguish — the bitterness — that has imprisoned you. Walk in that freedom. Take My Hand and walk with Me in that freedom. Let My Love wash away the pain."

Jan. 30

You are my hiding place;
You will protect me from trouble and
surround
me with songs of deliverance.
[PSALM 32:7]

"When you are down, and depressed, turn to Me. Bow down, pour out your heart to Me, cry — or cry out. Then worship Me for Who I am. When you are down, think how long it has been since you worshipped Me, or surrounded yourself with songs of praise? Spiritual songs turn your heart to worship Me, and give thanks to Me. — Give thanks to Me for even the smallest thing. It will lift the gloom, and turn your mourning into dancing. I will give you songs of deliverance, to deliver you from your **self**— your gloom — your pain — your fear. Worship and fear cannot co-exist. Fear is lack of trust in your All-Powerful Savior. Lift your heart in worship — and lift your head in trust — and joy will flood your heart."

Jan. 31

You were taught, with regard to your former way of life, to put off your old self, which is being corrupted by its deceitful desires, to be made new in the attitude of your minds.
[EPHESIANS 4:22-23]

"When you feel yourself slipping away from reality, into a dream world, or fantasy of 'I wish I . . .' — draw ever–closer to Me, in an atmosphere of worship, and you shall see that what you really need is Me. I AM — Ponder that — I AM. . . . But your flesh — your self — is speaking — is in control, when you think you desire earthly things, or you desire people who pull you away from Me, or even ministry that brings you glory. Who, then, is on the throne? Which kingdom do you serve? In which kingdom do you dwell? And at the end of this day, which ruler brings you deep joy? De-throne self. Turn to Me in worship, and be filled again with Joy, and Peace."

Feb. 1

Put on your new nature, and be renewed
as you learn to know your Creator
and become like Him.
[COLOSSIANS 3:10 (NLT)]

But as for me, it is good to be near God.
[PSALM 73:28a]

"With every shout of praise that you lift to Me — with every tear shed — you touch My Heart. And the washing of My Spirit cleanses you more and more. — With everything that draws you closer to Me, **self** is washed away more and more. — And I am enthroned on your heart on a deeper plane. Draw closer and closer to Me, and I will set you free — more and more free of **self**— so you will be fully Mine. Only then are you who I created you to be. Only then, can you be used in fullness. Pour out **self** and be flooded with Me — with My Spirit — with My Love — with My Presence — with My Purpose."

Feb. 2

You fill me with Joy in Your Presence, with eternal pleasures at Your Right Hand.
[PSALM 16:11b]

"The Essence of My Presence fills your heart with such Joy and Peace that you can no longer stand. The Essence and Presence of My Spirit and My Love and My Power overwhelm the enemy and set him fleeing. You are free. Now you are free, not only from sin and guilt and shame, but of fear — of **self** — of unrest — of despondency — of pain. And you are filled with Me — only Me — only My Love, My Peace, My Worth, My Joy and Freedom — Me — just Me."

Feb. 3

As a mother comforts her child,
so will I comfort you.
[ISAIAH 66:13a]

"You are Mine; I am yours ~~ yours to comfort you in times of sorrow or despair. Come sit at My Feet. I want to feed your weary soul. I am here for you ~~ at your beckoning call. Talk to Me. Tell Me your sorrows . . . your fears . . . your secrets . . . your desires . . . your dreams . . . your wants. . . . Pour it all out. . . . Lay every burden, every hope, at My Feet. Now, trust Me. Lean on Me, child. Rest your weary head. Soak up My Love . . . My Mercy . . . My Grace . . . My Peace . . . My Love ~~ My Lavish Love."

Feb. 4

He whose walk is blameless and who does what is righteous, who speaks the truth from his heart and has no slander on his tongue, who does his neighbor no wrong and casts no slur on his fellowman. . . . He who does these things will never be shaken.
[PSALM 15:2,3,5b]

Reckless words pierce like a sword, but the tongue of the wise brings healing.
[PROVERBS 12:18]

"There is great Power in the tongue! The tongue needs taming. You can speak blessings. — You can speak curses. Each has Powerful effects!! Speaking blessings over others brings My Riches into action in their lives. But speaking curses brings destruction. Speaking curses is often done unknowingly — and those curses are then open doors for the enemy to enter that life and set up destruction. Speak only life into others. Let nothing negative come off your tongue. You know not the destruction that can then ensue, when the enemy has free range in that person's life — in your own life. So often, negative thoughts are proclaimed, unknowingly opening the door to the enemy. Make a vow right now, to train your tongue to speak no negative curses — no negative thoughts — of a brother or sister, especially. Do unto others as you would have them do unto you. Set up a standard against the enemy by changing those curses into blessings. You are My agent of war-fare against the enemy when you rebuke — when you revoke — those curses, and speak blessings. Be My agent of change."

Feb. 5

Ask where the good way is, and walk in it,
and you will find rest for your soul.
[JEREMIAH 6:16b]

"You are a child of the King. Watch and wait and you will see the Glory of the LORD displayed in your life — in your midst. Come to Me and I will set you free from the heavy burdens you carry. My Yoke is easy and My burden is light — I carry it for you. I only allow you — I only expect you — to carry what you can carry. I do not burden you. I allow earth's burdens to weigh you down no more than you can handle as you grow in My Strength and you depend more and more on My Strength to carry you through. Watch and wait, and you will find rest for your soul."

Feb. 6

His master replied, "Well done, good and faithful servant! Come and share your master's happiness."
[MATTHEW 25:21a,c,23a,c]

"Dear child, remember — call to mind — the moments when you have heard Me say, 'Well done!' When you are weary — or feeling shame, or remorse — or you are fearful to take the next step — recall My WORDS, 'Well done!' And take comfort in knowing you have pleased Me, and brought Me Joy, in times past. Repent of turning away — yes — but then, know you are washed clean of those spots and blemishes and filthy rags. You are then free to walk in freedom — to do My Bidding once again. Press on to bigger victories — more Powerful ministry — more intimate oneness with Me. Then hear Me say once again, 'Well done!'"

Feb. 7

I am the Vine; you are the branches. If a man remains in Me and I in Him, he will bear much fruit; apart from Me you can do nothing.
This is to My Father's Glory,
that you bear much fruit,
showing yourselves to be My disciples.
[JOHN 15:5,8a]

But the fruit of the Spirit is love, joy, peace, patience, kindness, goodness, faithfulness, gentleness and self-control.
[GALATIANS 5:22-23]

"I am the Vine. You are the branches — pruned to bear much fruit — more plentiful with each season of growth. Bearing good fruit is the mark of My faithful followers — who are fed by the Vine in more and more succulent measure. Draw Life and be nourished by the succulent flow from the Vine. Be fed in ever-increasing measure, as you grow and flourish. Bear fruit in ever-increasing measure as you draw Life and Living Water from the Vine."

Feb. 8

Blessed are those who have learned to acclaim You, who walk in the Light of Your Presence, O LORD.
[PSALM 89:15]

"The Light of My Presence is upon you. The Light of My Presence is upon you to speak Freedom to the captives, Love to My Bride, Love to the lonely — the brokenhearted — the needy. What each needs is Me. — What each needs is My Love — My intimacy — My Presence — My Power . . . in their lives — in their hearts — in their relationships — in their homes."

Feb. 9

"In the last days," God says,
"I will pour out My Spirit on all people.
Your sons and daughters will prophesy, your
young men will see visions, your old men
will dream dreams.
Even on My servants, both men and women,
I will pour out My Spirit in those days, and
they
will prophesy."
[ACTS 2:17-18]

Let us rejoice and be glad and give Him
Glory!
For the wedding of the Lamb has come, and
His bride has made herself ready.
[REVELATION 19:7]

"I am bringing a Wave of My Spirit over this nation — calling My bride to her feet — to be ready to meet her Groom. She must be fully clothed in My Garment of Praise to be fully adorned and fully protected on the day of My Coming. Awaken My bride to the Fullness of My Spirit being poured out on her. Be My agents of transformation as you join up with other believers who are now filled with My Spirit — My Power. Awaken My Bride to the fullness of Joy that shall be hers in days to come — in all of eternity."

Feb. 10

Do not be afraid or discouraged. . . .
For the battle is not yours, but God's.
[2 CHRONICLES 20:15]

"You are Mine. No foe can defeat you. Believe that. Live like you believe it. Cast out fear and the sense of failure at once — at every turn — until you know — until you sense — the battle is Mine. My Forces always win — making you the victor!"

Feb. 11

Come near to God and He will come near to you.
[JAMES 4:8a]

Look to the LORD and His Strength;
Seek His Face always.
[PSALM 105:4]

"Give Me your moments. You can companion with Me all throughout your day. As you do your work, let Me walk beside you in Divine Companionship. Then, and then alone, will you hear My gentle leading, and experience My Love for you in all the little things in your day. When you ignore Me and fail to recognize My Presence there with you, you lose so much of Me that I want you to know of Me and receive from Me ~~ so you can grow like Me. Love Me. Rest in Me. Talk to Me. Listen to Me. Joy in Me. Learn from Me. Turn to Me. Be changed by Me. . . . Give Me your moments."

Feb. 12

My Presence will go with you,
and I will give you rest.
[EXODUS 33:14]

"Come to Me, child, and I will give you rest — rest for your soul, your heart, your mind. Then, turn, and follow Me — turn, and worship Me — turn, and love Me. — — Abundance of Life-giving Tenderness and Mercy and Love are awaiting you to claim. Claim it, child. Claim My Presence, My Power, My Strength, My Love, My Tender Mercies. You are in My Great Care. Nothing can harm you if you will stay by My Side and claim My Power to save you from all harm and enemy control. Flee from your humanly sinful nature. Come running to Me, and I will set you free — free from **self** — free from sin's stronghold on you. You are Mine. — Walk as if you are Mine. Flee the enemy camp. Join Hands with Me, and I will set you free."

Feb. 13

I am the LORD, the God of all mankind.
Is anything too hard for Me?
[JEREMIAH 32:27]

Do not fear, for I am with you; do not be
dismayed, for I am your God.
I will strengthen you and help you; I will
uphold you with My Righteous Right Hand.
[ISAIAH 41:10]

I love the LORD, for He heard my voice;
He heard my cry.
[PSALM 116:1]

"I hear you, child. I hear the cry of your heart. Come to Me out of love, out of need, out of joy and thanksgiving. Whatever your need — whatever your praise — I am listening. — I am here. — I will save and provide. Come to Me and I will give you . . . whatever your needs are today. See, child, I am your All in All — — All Love — All-Sufficient — All-Powerful — always present — always near. Come close to Me, and I will be your Lover, your Healer, your Provider, your . . . — to fulfill your every need — to find Joy in your praise . . . your love."

Feb. 14

Consider the Great Love of the LORD.
[PSALM 107:43b]

How precious is Your Lovingkindness, O God!
How priceless is Your unfailing Love!
[PSALM 36:7a (NASB)/(NIV)]

"When your heart is hurting for love, come to Me. When your heart is brimming over with love to share, come to Me ~~ your First Love. I created you with a desire to love and be loved. When you first ran to My Arms for cleansing and forgiveness, I showered you with My Unfailing Love ~~ My Tender Loving-kindnesses. And for the first time, you knew what True Love is. Come back to your First Love. Your heart is empty and cold when you leave your First Love. But come running to Me more and more, and your capacity to love and be loved shall deepen. Come running to Me in Love."

Feb. 15

God disciplines us for our good, that we may share in His Holiness.
No discipline seems pleasant at the time, but painful.
Later on, however, it produces a harvest of righteousness and peace for those who have been trained by it.
[HEBREWS 12:10b,11]

"Child, recognize that the training you have endured has brought growth, and progress, in the training of your soul to love Me more and more. The imperfections in your character you recognize now are what, before the training, you could not see. The world clouds them. My Light reveals them. The closer you get to Me, the more you see your imperfections and failures. But, child, recognizing the flaws in character you see now, is evidence of a closer walk with Me ~~ a deepening love for Me. For you to see them, and feel such remorse, is the mark of growth. So take comfort, child. The refining fire brings forth purer gold."

Feb. 16

*I will listen to what God the LORD will say;
He promises Peace to His people.*
[PSALM 85:8a]

"I have WORDS for you to hear each day. Open the ears of your heart and listen ~~ quietly, and at rest ~~ listen. It is then you will hear My quiet WORDS, spoken just for you. Listen, child. I am here. Be still and know that I am God, Who speaks WORDS of Grace, of Correction, of Guidance, of My Kingdom Treasures. Come unto Me and I will give you rest. Come, child, sit at My Feet. Be humble, be listening, be used. I love you, child. You are Mine. Sit with Me, and My Presence will alter your inner being. Sit with Me, and I will give you Peace. Sit with Me, and I will fill you with My Power, My, Love, My Truths. Now, rest ~~ rest in My Arms of Love ~~ and listen."

Feb. 17

All the king's officials and the people of the royal provinces know that for any man or woman who approaches the king in the inner court without being summoned the king has but one law: that he be put to death. The only exception to this is for the king to extend the gold scepter to him and spare his life.
[ESTHER 4:11]

"Be filled with My Spirit — more and more. Come to Me — more and more. Love on Me, and be Loved — more and more. Come to Me, and I will give you My Love — My Beauty — My Bounty — My Freedom — My Joy. I extend My Golden Scepter to you. Take My Hand, and follow Me into My Kingdom — deeper and deeper into My Inner Courts. Then will you be truly Mine — Mine to Love, to nurture, to cherish."

Feb. 18

I pray that out of His Glorious Riches He may strengthen you with Power through His Spirit in your inner being, so that Christ may dwell in your heart through faith.
[EPHESIANS 3:16,17a]

"Hear My WORDS of Life — spoken to your tender heart. Open the doors of your heart — that I may enter, and dwell with you, and draw you into a more intimate relationship with Me. Be alert to My Leading, My Guidance. I will take you along the path I have prepared for you. Awaken, My child, and come with Me."

Feb. 19

*Satisfy us in the morning with
Your Unfailing Love.*
[PSALM 90:14a]

"Trust Me, child, I will bring you through the storms and gales, and twists and turns of life. Run to Me for this sweet time alone with Me, where you can gain rest for your mind and soul — and find comfort and tender fellowship. You long for that. Seek Me early. Then your day will be ordered aright. Be still and know Me — know Me more deeply each time you come to Me in this time of sweet intercourse of our spirits. Come to Me early, child, and I will give you rest, and fill you once again with My Presence, My Spirit, My Love. Rest in My Arms. Be still, and know Me more deeply, each time we come together like this. I love you, child."

Feb. 20

Therefore God exalted Him to the highest place
and gave Him the Name that
is above every name,
that at the Name of Jesus every knee should
bow,
in heaven and on earth and under the
earth.
[PHILIPPIANS 2:9-10]

"Yes, My Name — Jesus — use it often, to dispel all gloom, all fear, all temptation, all dread, all weariness, all pain — both emotional and physical pain — all evil thoughts toward others, all despair, all loneliness. Recognize those evils that lurk around you — working to destroy you, and to draw you away from Me. Then, just say My Name, 'Jesus.' And all evil must flee. Use it often. It is for freedom that I came to set you free. Walk in that freedom from evil oppression. — When you say My Name lovingly, prayerfully, tenderly, powerfully, watch the enemy flee. It is by My Name that you are saved and set free. Use it often. Use it freely. Then, lean on Me and I will gather you into My Arms, and put you at rest, put your soul at peace, fill your heart with My Love."

Feb. 21

I guide you in the Way of Wisdom and lead you along straight paths.
[PROVERBS 4:11]

"Lay **self** aside, and do My Bidding. Then you will know that freedom, for which I came to set you free. Watch, wait for My Leading, then go — or stay, and pray — or communicate with those I lead you to touch. It is never the same. Do not make your service for Me a habitual ritual. It is new every morning. Listen, and obey."

Feb. 22

In Your Unfailing Love You will lead the people
You have redeemed.
In Your Strength You will guide them.
[EXODUS 15:13]

"Go in Peace. I will lead you and guide you along your way. My Love will set you free — free from weariness — free from worry — free from fear — free from bondage. Take My Hand, child, and walk with Me."

Feb. 23

Humble yourselves, therefore,
under God's Mighty Hand,
that He may lift you up in due time.
[1 PETER 5:6]

For He chose us in Him before
the creation of the world
to be holy and blameless in His Sight.
In Love He predestined us to be adopted as
His sons through Jesus Christ, in accordance
with
His Pleasure and Will—to the praise of His
Glorious Grace, which He has freely given us.
[EPHESIANS 1:4-6]

"Do as I command, and you will remain in My Love. You are My child. I adopted you into My Kingdom. You were formed in My Heart long before you had life — My Life flowing through you. You are a child of Me — your King. Come, bow down in awe and wonder of the Majesty of My Throne. Bow down, and humble yourself. In due time, I will lift you up."

Feb. 24

The Name of the LORD is a Strong Tower; the righteous run to it and are safe.
[PROVERBS 18:10]

See, the Sovereign LORD comes with Power, and His Arm rules for Him. He tends His flock like a shepherd: He gathers the lambs in His Arms and carries them close to His heart. He gently leads those that have young.
[ISAIAH 40:10a,11]

"Sit with Me. Listen to Me. Learn of Me. Be refreshed by My Spirit. In My Arms is Everlasting Peace. In My Arms you will be secure and at rest. In My Arms is Everlasting Love. In My Arms you are safe, child. Run to Me. Rest in My Arms. Cling to Me. I am Your Strong Tower. Run to Me and you are safe. Cling to Me and you are fed. Rest in My Arms and you are filled with My Spirit and surrounded by My Love."

Feb. 25

I trust in Your Unfailing Love.
[PSALM 13:5a]

"You are My child. I Love you dearly. Claim My Love. Claim My Power to overcome the disappointments and pain. I endured them for you. I know your pain. I feel your tears on My Shoulder as I hold you tightly to My Bosom. Rest in My Arms. Be at Peace."

Feb. 26

Freedom is what we have — Christ has set us free! Stand, then, as free people.
[GALATIANS 5:1 (GNT)]

"Yes, child, I have set you free. Walk in that freedom. Lay that burden at My Feet, and experience that Perfect Release from sin and death. — Rise to new heights with Me. Come, child. Come and let Me set you free from the hurt, the pain, the shame, the fear. It is for freedom that I came to set you free. Walk in that freedom — released from the woes of this world. Soar with Me to new heights. Cling to Me. . . . I give you complete release."

Feb. 27

May the God of Hope fill you with all Joy and Peace as you trust in Him, so that you may overflow with Hope by the Power of the Holy Spirit.
[ROMANS 15:13]

"I long to give you My Joy and Gladness. When you are at rest within your spirit — within your heart — and you are open to My Gentle Touch, then My Joy can ripple through you — even when times are rough. Lean on Me. . . . Trust Me. . . . Sense My Love. . . . My Joy will flood your heart, when you are at rest within you."

Feb. 28

I have stilled and quieted my soul.
[PSALM 131:2a]

"You are a source of My Joy to the lost and hurting and lonely — when you open your heart to Me, and then walk in such a way that My Light shines through you — when you hear Me speak, and pass My WORDS, My Love, on to those around you, and those dear ones in your heart. Child, hear My Voice speak deep Truths to you. Then wait in silence until your heart is at peace, and your soul at rest. It is then that you have shut out the worldly influences around you, and you commune intimately with Me — rejoicing in thankfulness for all I have been doing for you — in you — through you. You are My friend. Wait for My Counsel, then act and speak according to My Will for you. Sit at rest — in the quiet hush of My Spirit at work in you. I love you. Rest now in My Loving Arms."

Feb. 29

But as for me, I am filled with Power, with the Spirit of the LORD.
[MICAH 3:8a]

"Trust in Me — My Miracle-working Power. — Stand firm and use that Power to overcome the attacks of the enemy. You are more than a conqueror through Me — through My Power. Walk on in confidence, knowing My Spirit, Who raised Christ from the dead, goes with you — lives within you. Rest in that Almighty Power — that Almighty Tender Love."

March 1

And God said, "Let there be. . . ."
And there was.
[GENESIS 1:3,5,6,8,14,19]

"I take Joy in seeing you take delight in My creation — the Great Wonders of My Mighty Hand — the Production by My Voice at the beginning of time. As you take delight in the beauty, the colors, the delicacies, the majesty — take greater delight in the Master Designer Who set it all in motion. One Word from My Lips begat all you see — and more. Be equally awed by My Hand at work even now as Mightily — as Greatly — as Awesomely. — Each flower, each baby, each sunrise, each sunset, each rainbow, each flash of lightening, each snowflake, each . . .— all done by the Work of My Hand. See Me in each creation. — Even in the faces of those around you. — Even in the face of the one reflected in the mirror. See Me at work — in your heart — yes — but also, in your smile, your tears — yes, even your tears."

March 2

Seek peace and pursue it.
[PSALM 34:14b]

Now may the LORD of Peace Himself give you Peace at all times and in every way.
[2 THESSALONIANS 3:16]

I will listen to what God the LORD will say; He promises Peace to His people.
[PSALM 85:8a]

"Seek My Peace, and find it — find it as you lay your burdens down at My Feet. You live in a world of unrest and a hurried pace. Seek My Peace — My Calming Balm of Gilead — as you sit with Me, and drink from My Well of Living Water — My Refreshing Life-giving Water. Come, child, kneel at My Feet, drink deeply . . . restfully. . . . Wait expectantly."

March 3

But as for me, it is good to be near God.
[PSALM 73:28a]

"Child, your heart is linked tightly to Mine. I reveal My hidden Truths to you, that you may be a beacon of My Light to a broken world. My Presence is near ~~ is surrounding you ~~ filling you even now. Go forth unafraid. My Presence is always available to you. My Presence is always near. Walk in it."

March 4

Trust in the LORD with all your heart and
lean not on your own understanding.
[PROVERBS 3:5]

"Child, lean on Me when your world starts crashing in on you. Lean on My Strength, My Loving Arms, My Wisdom, My Peace. Lay your burdens down at My Feet. Lean on Me to work out the details. Listen for My Lead, then, to proceed according to My Will — My Path — My Plan for you. I love you, child. Lean on that Truth — that Promise."

March 5

In my anguish I cried to the LORD, and He answered by setting me free. Let those who fear the LORD say, "His Love endures forever."
[PSALM 118:5,4]

"When you are weakest — and you admit your weaknesses — I can then be at My Strongest for you. Whether it is an attack of the enemy — or whether it is failure on your part — I can be your Strong Tower — your Rampart in these times of trouble. I will hold you in the Palm of My Hand through the battle — and carry you under My Wings — to spare you the shame and the harm — or, to strengthen you because of it. Your character is molded more and more, with every life lesson — if you humble yourself and pray, and seek My Face . . . My Strength . . . My Love . . . My Power . . . My Mercy . . . My Compassion . . . My All. And then, if you can bow at My Feet, and worship Me — the process is complete. Lean into My Embrace. I Love you, child. You are Mine — that is what gives you worth. Go forth unafraid. The battle is Mine now. Go forth with Praise on your lips, Joy in your heart, Release in your soul. You are now — once again — set free. Go forth with Praise. Now you can be an unblocked channel of My Love, My Mercy, My Grace — to the world around you. Go forth with Praise on your lips, and My Love in your heart."

March 6

Do not be afraid.
Stand firm and you will see the deliverance
the LORD will bring you today.
The LORD will fight for you;
you need only be still.
[EXODUS 14:13a,14]

The LORD is close to the brokenhearted and
saves those who are crushed in spirit.
[PSALM 34:18]

This is the one I esteem:
he who is humble and contrite in spirit,
and trembles at My Word.
[ISAIAH 66:2]

"That you show remorse at all is a sign of maturity. See it as one step closer to Me. I set the enemy fleeing and set you free from his attack when you humble yourself like this to Me. Each time you enter My Holy of Holies draws your heart closer to Mine. If My people will humble themselves and pray and seek My Face, I will extend My Healing Hand, and touch those secret places in each heart, in each mind, in each soul, in each spirit ~~ healing those broken hearts, healing those sin-sick souls, healing those wounded spirits."

March 7

No one knows the Thoughts of God except the
Spirit of God.
We have not received the spirit of the world
but the Spirit Who is from God.
We have the mind of Christ.
[1 CORINTHIANS 2:11b,12,16b]

You received the Spirit of Sonship. And by
Him we cry, "Abba Father."
[ROMANS 8:15b]

"See to it, child, to set your mind fully on Me. — One with Me. — That is the reward. Have the Mind of Christ, and you have the Mind of a Son. That Son's Thoughts were always on Me. He is your Example. The Spirit of Sonship begins with this: Have the mind of Christ, My son."

March 8

Love the LORD your God with all your heart
and with all your soul and
with all your strength.
[DEUTERONOMY 6:5]

You will fill me with Joy in Your Presence,
with eternal pleasures at Your Right Hand.
[PSALM 16:11b]

Thanks be to God, Who always leads us in
triumphal procession in Christ and through
us spreads everywhere the fragrance of the
knowledge of Him.
[2 CORINTHIANS 2:14]

"You are Mine. You do not realize how it touches My Heart for you to come to Me like this ~~ to sit at My feet ~~ to embrace Me ~~ to take My Hand. Just sit at My Feet and drop your burdens down, and be set free to pour out your love and adoration. ~~ Just love on Me, and then there is no way you will not sense My Presence, My Love, My Abundance. I love you, child. Sit with Me, embraced by My Love, embraced by My Presence. Then, go in Peace. You will be a sweet fragrance to those you encounter."

March 9

Oh LORD, truly I am Your servant . . . You have freed me from my chains.
[PSALM 116:16]

"I am yours — your King and your God. Look to Me. Together we form a team to take down the enemy, and loose the chains around those you love, who are still held captive by the enemy — by this world — as you once were. They are hurting, and need to be set free to become Mine. Be now My servant and the conduit of My Love, My Life, My Freedom, when you join hands with Me, to loose those chains that bind them. Work with Me. I want to use you as I set them free from their chains to become My servants."

March 10

*"For I know the plans I have for you,"
declares the LORD, "plans to prosper you and
not to harm you, plans to give you hope and
a future."*
[JEREMIAH 29:11]

"Child, you are My treasured possession. Every day I want to hold you close ~~ for you to feel the Heartbeat of My Spirit flowing from Me, into your heart. Fix your eyes, your thoughts, your heart on Me. I am your Dearest Friend. I know the plans I have for you ~~ plans to give you a rich future ~~ full of Life ~~ My Life, My Spirit, My Presence. Run away with Me from the cares of this world. You are Mine. I set you free when you take My Hand and follow Me."

March 11

The LORD is near to all who call on Him.
[PSALM 146:18a]

"I love to give gifts and special training to those who understand and find joy in receiving those gifts — that special training — the gentle bending — to create a soul that desires to do My Will. I desire the companionship of those dear souls that have given themselves totally to Me. I treasure our Friendship. I want you closer and closer to Me. I want our eyes to meet more often. . . . Ponder those thoughts."

March 12

O God, You are My God, earnestly I seek You;
my soul thirsts for You, my body longs for
You.
Because Your Love is better than life,
my lips will glorify You.
I will praise You as long as I live, and in
Your Name I will lift up my hands.
[PSALM 63:1a,3,4]

"Praise Me and lift Me up, to shine My Light into your midst, so there is no space for the enemy to dwell. Humble yourself before Me; come humbly to My Throne where you may sit at My Feet and find Comfort, and Joy, and Love, and the washing of My Spirit. Feel My Touch, and know My Power is working for your good in everything. Be captivated by My Love, My Presence, My Power, My Glory, My Peace. Sit here at rest, child. Be empty of self, and be cleansed by the Power of My Spirit, that raised Christ from the dead. That Power is available to you at all times, when your heart is linked to Mine. Appropriate that Power. Use it for My Glory. Take My Hand and be empty of self. — Only then can you use that Power to change you — to change the world around you. Grasp My Hand, and now listen for My Voice to lead you on from here."

March 13

You will fill me with joy in Your Presence.
[ACTS 2:28b]

Then I heard the Voice of the LORD saying,
"Whom shall I send?
And who will go for us?" And I said, "Here
am I. Send me!"
[ISAIAH 6:8]

"Put **self** to rest. Have no thoughts. Just sit in My Presence. ~~ Let the world around you vanish. Listen for My Still Small Voice that gets lost in all the noise in this world. Be still. Be alert only to My Spirit. Hear My Spirit call your name. Then, be willing to respond, 'Here am I. Send me.'"

March 14

How precious to me are Your Thoughts, O God!
[PSALM 139:17a]

"Take care, child, to do My Bidding, once you hear My Call. You greatly anticipate My Words to you, and think what they might be. — — You are beginning to know my Thoughts — My Tender Thoughts — My Plans for you. You are My precious child, My servant, My friend. I love you and want you near Me. Come, child. Sit at My Feet. Let your tears flow as you hear My Words to you. Leave your fears and anxious thoughts here with Me. Take care to do My Bidding."

March 15

Do you not know that your body is the temple (the very sanctuary) of the Holy Spirit Who lives within you?
[1 CORINTHIANS 6:19a (AMP)]

"When you come to be alone with Me like this, I must have your total devotion, for Me to reveal these hidden Truths to you. Your senses must be turned off ~~ for you to enter My Presence, where your spirit joins with My Spirit~~ to hear Me whisper these Truths to you. Child, absorb the Beauty of My Love for you ~~ My very deep, compassionate Love for you. Turn to Me in your inner being ~~ clothed in My Robe of Righteousness ~~ alone with Me here in your secret place. You now can enter My throne room. When you enter My Presence like this, you are a temple of My Spirit. ~~ Your heart is My throne room ~~ My inner Holy of Holies, when your heart is in total surrender to Me ~~ when you have made Me King and Sovereign Ruler over your life, over your heart, your thoughts, your secret places. Bow down. ~~ Bow down in total surrender ~~ totally immersed in My Redeeming Love ~~ totally at one with Me."

March 16

Be still and know that I am God.
[PSALM 46:10a]

"For I know the Plans I have for you,"
declares the LORD.
[JEREMIAH 29:11a]

O Sovereign LORD, You are God!
Your Words are trustworthy,
and You have promised these good
things to Your servant.
[2 SAMUEL 7:28]

"Submit to My Leadership. I know the Plans I have for you. . . .I will see them through. Be still. Be held. Be led. Be free. Know that I AM God. I am here. Trust Me."

March 17

Yours, O LẑRD, is the Greatness and the
Power and the Glory and the Majesty and
the Splendor, for everything
in heaven and earth is Yours.
Yours, O LẑRD, is the Kingdom; You are
exalted
as Head over all.
[1 CHRONICLES 29:11]

"When you claim My Power to move — and then you act — empowered by Me — you will put into motion Mighty Acts of War against the enemy, and bring Victory to your acts of kindness and love. Go forth — directed only by Me. Take My Hand and let Me lead you on to victory. I love you! Claim My Power! Go forth and claim My Power!"

March 18

*I will remain in the world no longer,
but they are still in the world,
and I am coming to You.
Holy Father, protect them by the Power of
Your Name — the Name You gave Me.*
[JOHN 17:11]

"All Power is given to Me! I am your Healer — your Provider. All Power is given to My Name! That at the very utterance of My Name, the enemy must flee. Say it often: 'JESUS!' Say it in faith — in trust of Me. ALL POWER is given to Me — your Healer. Pain, disease, infirmity must flee at My Name — JESUS. ALL POWER is given to that Name. Say it often. Say it in faith. Say it in trust of your ALMIGHTY King — JESUS!!!! . . . Now . . . out of love . . . out of quiet love . . . say it, 'Jesus.'"

March 19

Know that the LORD has set apart
the godly for Himself.
[PSALM 4:3a]

"Child, know that My one true assignment for you is for your life to speak My Words to others around you ~~ to be My Voice, My Hands, My Feet. I set you apart for Myself. Lean on Me. Lean on My Love, My Power, My Forgiveness, My Mercy, My Grace, My Peace! And be filled with My Joy as you bring Me Glory and Honor, in so doing."

March 20

*Glorious and Majestic are His Deeds, and His
Righteousness endures forever.*
[PSALM 111:13]

*Yet the LORD longs to be gracious to you;
He rises to show you Compassion.*
[ISAIAH 30:18a]

Serve one another in love.
[GALATIANS 5:13b]

"I am God Almighty, Maker of heaven and earth, King
over all the universe, Creator of all things, Glorious
and Majestic — and yet, I know your name; I heal your
wounds; I know your every need; I hear each cry of your
heart; I see each tear; I know and have felt every pain,
every injury, each breaking of your heart; I have forgiven
your every sin. And, I use you for My Glory. I use you
to wipe away tears, touch wounded spirits, encourage
the broken-hearted, bring Joy and Peace to the weary,
embrace and comfort the mourner, give generously to
the needy, touch little children from broken homes, share
My Truth with this broken world. . . .And I cherish your
whispers of love — your songs of praise — your tears of
Joy over My Touch, My Embrace, My Love."

March 21

The Eyes of the LORD are on those who fear Him, on those whose hope is in His Unfailing Love.
[PSALM 33:18]

"Child, I will hold your hand and lead you along the way ~~ just as I have, when you turned to Me in times of trouble, in times of need, in times of thanksgiving. . . . Turn your face toward Me. . . . And when our eyes meet, lay back in My Arms, and let My Strength ~~ My Rest ~~ My Peace ~~ My Love ~~ permeate your very being."

March 22

Be self-controlled and alert. Your enemy the devil prowls around like a roaring lion looking for someone to devour. Resist him, standing firm in the faith.
[1 PETER 5:8,9a]

I have come into the world as a Light, so that no one who believes in Me should stay in darkness.
[JOHN 12:46]

"Be strong in My Power, full of love and zeal and hope. Use My Word to set you free from the ways of this world. Stand on the Solid Rock — your Firm Foundation. Be at peace. Shine My Light into the darkness around you. If you cannot shine My Light, the darkness will consume you and cloud your thoughts. Beware of all evil, all darkness. You are My child, so darkness has no control over you — unless you let it. Stand firm. Do not give the enemy a foothold. He has no power over you — unless you allow it."

March 23

Fear of man will prove to be a snare,
but whoever trusts in the LORD is kept safe.
[PROVERBS 29:25]

Let the beloved of the LORD rest secure in
Him,
for He shields him all the day long.
[DEUTERONOMY 33:12a]

"Dispel fear at all costs. You cannot, you will not, accomplish My Work, My Will, if you are fearful. Say My Name. Say it often. Allow Me to wrap you in My Perfect Love. Then it is that you will know you are protected, and at peace, and at rest in your inner being. By My Name — at rest in My Perfect Love — those fears will be cast out — never to return unless you let them. Let My Perfect Love cast out all your fears. — And your growing, deepening love for Me will grow stronger."

March 24

Wealth and honor come from You;
You are Ruler of all things.
In Your Hands are Strength and Power to
exalt and give Strength to all.
[1 CHRONICLES 29:12]

Summon Your Power, O God; show us Your
Strength, O God, as You have done before.
[PSALM 68:28]

The thief comes only to steal and kill
and destroy;
I came that you may have life, and have it
abundantly.
[JOHN 10:10 (NASB)]

"Claim My Power when your strength and courage fail you. My Power will never fail you. Claim it, child. Claim it often. How I love to display My Power in My servants' lives!! Too often, though, I am shut out by **self** and things of this world. Claim My Power, and live an Abundant Life. — That Abundant Life is available to My friends at all times. Come into My Presence and commune with Me. Claim My Power, My Love, My Peace; then will you step into that Realm of My Abundant, Supernatural Plenty. Walk with Me in My Garden of Plenty. Then go out into the world, coming back into My Secret Place whenever evil lurks — whenever **self** reappears."

March 25

But as for me, it is good to be near God.
I have made the Sovereign LORD my refuge.
[PSALM 73:28]

"Draw near to Me. Make that your focus ~~ nearer to Me today than yesterday. You will be changed ~~ continually transformed. Come into My Presence ~~ in the ultimate of intimacy with Me ~~ your Maker, Defender, Redeemer ~~ your nearest, dearest Friend. Think of it ~~ intimate friend of the King of the Universe ~~ union with your Prince of Peace ~~ your Master, Redeemer ~~ your Friend. Bask in My Presence. Treasure these times together. You will be changed."

March 26

It is for freedom that Christ has set us free.
Stand firm, then, and do not let yourselves
be burdened again by a yoke of slavery.
[GALATIANS 5:1]

Take My Yoke upon you and learn from Me,
for I am Gentle and Humble in Heart, and
you will find rest for your souls.
[MATTHEW 11:29]

We were therefore buried with Him through
baptism into death in order that, just as
Christ was raised from the dead through
the Glory of the Father,
we too may live a new life.
[ROMANS 6:4]

"Child, this is My Will for you — die to **self**, and rise with New Life — with new Love to share, with My Joy to pass on to the heavy-hearted. Be Mine. Be My constant companion. Die to **self**. Live your new life, with Me on the throne of your heart. Be set free from the ruler of this world — no longer burdened with the yoke of bondage to this world. Be set free to do My Will, and in so doing, come into union with Me. New Life awaits."

March 27

*But as for me, I am filled with Power,
with the Spirit of the LORD.*
[MICAH 3:8a]

*Because Jesus lives forever, He has a
permanent Priesthood. Therefore He is able
to save completely those who come to God
through Him, because He always
lives to intercede for them.*
[HEBREWS 7:24-25]

*Then you will know the Truth, and the Truth
will set you free.*
[JOHN 8:32]

"Stop listening to the lies of the enemy. You are not worthless in My Eyes! You are not powerless! You are Mine. That is what gives you worth. I am your Lover, your Protector, your Supply. It is My Touch you need. It is My Touch that gives you Power. It is My Touch that gives you worth. Come! Let Me touch you and fill you with Power — My Power — My Power that is Mighty to Save — to save you from you — from **self** — from slavery, from sin, from brokenness, from bondage, from fear, from impurity, from lies and condemnation of the enemy. Come unto Me when you are weary, weak, burdened, broken. I WILL set you free!"

March 28

I pray that out of His Glorious Riches He may strengthen you with Power through His Spirit in your inner being, so that Christ may dwell in your hearts through faith. And I pray that you, being rooted and established in love, may have power, together with all the saints, to grasp how wide and long and high and deep is the Love of Christ, and to know this Love that surpasses knowledge ~~ that you may be filled to the measure of all the fullness of God.
[EPHESIANS 3:16-19]

"No child of Mine should have an empty heart. The more you know Me, the closer your walk with Me, the more you see My Heart of Love, the more you will be filled with Me ~~ with My Love, My Power, My Strength. Come to Me, and I will give you the Treasures of My Heart, and of My Kingdom. Come close, child. Come close."

March 29

Hear my prayer, O God; listen to the Words of My Mouth.
[PSALM 54:2]

"Speak to Me, child. I am listening. The exact words are of no account. I know your heart. But yes, the Power of Prayer is in the way you release My Spirit to do My Work in your life, and the lives of others. Attune your spirit to My Spirit's Guidance. Be humble, and then your prayers are Mighty."

March 30

I have stilled and quieted my soul; like a
weaned child with its mother.
[PSALM 131:2]

"Sit with Me, child, and I will reveal to you the wonders of My Great Love. Trust and obey, at the sound of My Voice. I am Ever-Present, always near. Take comfort in My Arms of Love. I hear the cry of your heart. Trust Me to answer those cries with My Great Wisdom. I am always here for you. Lean on Me. Learn from Me. Wait with Me ~~ still and humble. . . . Still and humble. I love you, child. Be at peace."

March 31

*How great is the Love the
Father has lavished on us.*
[1 JOHN 3:1a]

*I have Loved you with an Everlasting Love;
I have drawn you with Loving-kindness.*
[JEREMIAH 31:3]

"You have heard Me say to you that I Love you with an
Everlasting Love. I draw you to Me with My Loving-
kindness being lavished on you. Rely on that. Sink deep
into the Truth, the Power, the sweetness of those WORDS."

April 1

*Encourage one another and build each
other up, just as in fact you are doing.*
[1 THESSALONIANS 5:11]

*I will be glad and rejoice in You; I will sing
praise to Your Name, O Most High.*
[PSALM 9:2]

"When someone gives you praise, or speaks a compliment to you, take it not with a spirit of vain conceit — take no pride in it. But turn it into a sweet joy-filled praise to Me for creating you — for forming you — for transforming you — into what caused delight in someone else's eyes — in someone else's heart. Humble yourself to accept their praise, with thanksgiving in your heart toward Me. Do not belittle the praise — or refuse it — and thus belittle or reject the giver. It will give them much joy in giving it if it is received with a joyful, humble heart. . . .Then, as you recall their special words, and think of the heart-touch it was for you, let it be a reminder — a wake-up call — to seek the good in others. Look for ways to lift others up — to sweeten someone else's day."

April 2

*I have hidden Your WORD in my heart that I might not sin against You.
Your WORD is a Lamp to my feet and a Light for my path.*
[PSALM 119:11,105]

"Sit still and know Me. Be still before Me, and know Me — know Me more intimately — more dearly. Keep My Commands. Know My WORD. Let it sink deep into your heart. Wrestle with it until it becomes yours — hidden in your heart — ready to be called on in your days of trouble. Let My WORDS be a Light unto your path — an Ever-present Help in times of darkness. My WORD — My Truth — sets miracles in motion. Claim that. Expect miracles — big miracles — and daily workings of My Spirit to cleanse you of all unrighteousness and failures. Be clean, child. Choose Me. Run first to My WORD — My Presence — My Truth — whenever failure besets you — temptations lure you — fear grips you. Then, it is, I can set you free from those worries . . . the pain . . . that fear. Then, it is, I can use you to set My Truth in motion — to enact My Miracle-Working Power. Hear My Voice. Cling to Me — to My WORD — to My Truth."

April 3

The LORD your God is with you,
He is Mighty to save.
He will take great delight in you, He will
quiet you with His Love.
[ZEPHANIAH 3:17]

"Child, is your heart disquieted within you? I now set My guardian angels round about you to protect you from the attacks of the enemy. Seek My Face. Fix your eyes, your thoughts on Me. Then, it is, child, that you will hear My Voice, and see My Miracle-Working Power at work in your life, in your heart. Be at rest in My Presence. Seek My Face and pursue it. Listen. Learn. Be touched. Be quieted with My Love. I do Love you, child. You are Mine."

April 4

The LORD confides in those who fear Him; He makes His Covenant known to them.
[PSALM 25:14]

Now if we are children, then we are heirs — heirs of God and co-heirs with Christ.
[ROMANS 8:17a]

"I will reveal to you the Secrets of My Kingdom — Secrets of living a Kingdom Life. But you must first enter into My Presence as a little child — humble, yet eager to receive My Gifts. Come near to Me. Come near. — That is the basis of Kingdom Living. The nearer you come to Me, the more I direct your steps. You are a co-heir with Christ of the Inheritance Treasures that await you. All Power available to Christ is now available to you — your free Gift to claim from the Treasures in your Inheritance. Claim it! Use it! Walk in it! — That Secret of Kingdom Living is experienced only by those who come near enough to Me to hear My Whispers. All Power available to Christ is now available to you, through My Spirit in your inner being. — Empowered by My Spirit. . . . Think on these things."

April 5

Teach me to do Your Will, for You are my God; may Your good Spirit lead me.
[PSALM 143:10]

"I may put people or activities or events in your pathway — unplanned detours to your day — for you to use the Spiritual Gifts I have given you — perhaps in answer to another's prayers. If you are open to My Lead, I then will use you to be My Hands — My Voice — My Tender Touch. However, if you are not open to follow My Lead . . . and you press on with your own agenda — ignoring My Lead — I must then use another willing soul, to do My Bidding. . . . Oh, child, think what blessings — what heart-touches you just missed."

April 6

He stilled the storm to a whisper; the waves of the sea were hushed.
[PSALM 107:29]

Look to the LORD and His Strength; seek His Face always.
[1 CHRONICLES 16:11]

I trust in Your Unfailing Love; My heart rejoices in Your Salvation.
[PSALM 13:5]

"In your most difficult moments, look to My Face. Take My Hand ~~ lean into My Embrace. Rest in My Peace. Drop your burdens at My Feet. Cast all your cares on Me. I am all you need. I will see you through the storm. I will provide for your every need. Wait. . . . Watch. . . . Trust Me at every turn. When you have lost your way, call out to Me. Praise Me in the storm. I will see you through it. Claim that Promise. Appropriate My Power ~~ to calm the raging sea ~~ to claim the answers you need ~~ to know which way to turn ~~ to put your fears to rest ~~ to trust Me to the end."

April 7

But in your hearts set apart Christ as LORD.
[1 PETER 3:15a]

"I want to be your LORD — not just your Savior, Redeemer — but your LORD — LORD of your life, LORD over your thoughts, your time, your relationships, your home, your laughter, your tears. I want to establish My Kingdom in your midst — enthroned on your heart — enthroned in your church — enthroned in this land. Speak it into existence: 'Jesus, I enthrone You on the throne of my heart, my life, my **self**.'

    — Child, it is finished. Now live, as if it is."

April 8

When I am afraid, I will trust in You.
In God, Whose Word I praise, in God I trust;
I will not be afraid.
[PSALM 56:3,4a]

"Over and over, I have heard you say to Me, 'LORD, I am so scared!! Help me!' Child, I am here! ~~ I am always here with you ~~ here to heal, to save, to set you free from fear and pain. Trust Me. Trust Me ~~ and all is well and good for you. You are at the making / breaking point. Trust Me. Declare your trust in Me. Go forward now, unafraid. Go forward, taking My Hand ~~ leaning on Me ~~ protected and safe in My Arms."

April 9

Come to Me, all you who are weary and burdened, and I will give you rest.
[MATTHEW 11:28]

How great is Your Goodness, which You have stored up for those who fear You. You hide them in the Secret Place of Your Presence from the conspiracies of man. You keep them secretly in a shelter from the strife.
[PSALM 31:19a,20 (NASB)]

"Lean on Me when you are tired and weary, weak and heavy-laden. And I will bring you rest and peace; I will guard you in My Secret Place — from all evil — from **self**."

April 10

Seek ye first the kingdom of God,
and His righteousness.
[MATTHEW 6:33 (KJV)]

Be still before the LORD
and wait patiently for Him.
[PSALM 37:7a]

"Seek ye first My Kingdom — My Righteousness. — —
And to that will be added My Presence . . . and My Voice
— whispering to your inner ears. Be still . . . and know My
Heart. Be still . . . and sense My Presence. Be still . . . and
feel My Tender Touch. Be still a few more moments. . . .
Rest in My Arms. . . . Let all your cares and burdens
drop. . . . Soak in My Peace . . . My Rest . . . My Love. . . .
Now, go in Peace, in freedom from all woe."

April 11

He has showed you, O man, what is good.
And what does the LORD require of you?
To act justly and to love mercy and to walk
humbly with your God.
[MICAH 6:8]

And we, who with unveiled faces all reflect
the LORD's Glory, are being transformed into
His likeness, with ever-increasing glory,
which comes from the LORD,
Who is the Spirit.
[2 CORINTHIANS 3:18]

"Keep in close contact with Me — nearer — ever nearer. And in so doing, you reflect Me, as you are continually being transformed into My likeness — My image of you seen through the Blood of the Lamb — perfect . . . sinless . . . righteous . . . just . . . pure and holy . . . compassionate . . . merciful . . . loving . . . forgiving. . . ."

April 12

He performs wonders that cannot be fathomed,
miracles that cannot be counted.
[JOB 5:9; 9:10]

Stretch out your hand to heal and perform
miraculous signs and wonders through the
Name of your Holy Servant Jesus.
[ACTS 4:30]

"Wonders have been — and yet still are — unfolding before you. Walk in that Light of My Kingdom, where My Miracle-Working Power is readily available to those whose hearts are fully set on Me — desiring only My Will, My Spirit, controlling all their ways. Child, you are one of My most treasured possessions, as you walk in My Ways — hand in Hand with Me. Now watch My Miracle-Working Power unfold before you — and operate in you and through you. Go forth in My Power."

April 13

In Your Unfailing Love you will lead the people
You have redeemed.
In Your Strength you will guide them.
[EXODUS 15:13]

I guide you in the way of wisdom and lead you along straight paths.
[PROVERBS 4:11]

My soul finds rest in God alone; my salvation comes from Him.
[PSALM 62:1]

"Trust Me, child, and I will lead you in the way you must go. I will give you strength in the battle, and wisdom to follow My Lead. The only way to find rest for your soul when the battle is raging is for you to follow My Lead. By My Hand, by My Unfailing Love, I will lead you when you trust Me. The battle is Mine. Your salvation comes from Me alone. Lean on My Strength in the battle. And find rest for your soul."

April 14

If you love Me, you will obey what I command.
[JOHN 14:15]

"Listen, child, and I will lead you by My Command. — Not just in the huge issues of life, but even in your smallest daily happenings. You know when you have not followed My leading — My Commands — because your heart and spirit are not at rest — and all is not well with your soul. Learn of Me. Follow Me. Obey me. And all will be well with your soul. Come to Me and rest at My Feet. Be strengthened; be set free, as you follow My Lead. I love you, child. Go in Peace."

April 15

*Teach me to do Your Will, for You are my God;
may Your good Spirit lead me on level ground.*
[PSALM 143:10]

"I hold you close to Me when your **self** does not push Me away. Feel My Gentle Touch. Learn from My Gentle Touch, that you are always in My care. Trust Me more fully. Lean on Me. Do not try to push Me down the pathway You want to go. Trust Me. I will answer the prayers of your heart in such a way as to lead you down the path I have chosen for you. Seek My Will. Watch and see how My Ways are only for your good and the good of those you love. Remember. . . I love them, too."

April 16

Therefore, as God's chosen people, holy and dearly loved, clothe yourselves with compassion, kindness, humility, gentleness and patience.
[COLOSSIANS 3:12]

Praise be to the God and Father of our LORD Jesus Christ, the Father of Compassion and the God of all comfort, Who comforts us in all our troubles, so that we can comfort those in any trouble with the comfort we ourselves have received from God.
[2 CORINTHIANS 1:3,4]

"You are My agent of Mercy. Therein lies your Power ~~ for those you love and reach out to ~~ to heal and comfort and protect them from the pain of this world. Be a channel of My Manifest Power ~~ an agent of Healing, Comfort, and Love. Never doubt that I can use you. In fact, when you feel at your weakest, that is when you may possibly be My strongest force of change ~~ when you can be the most humble channel of My Power. Those hurting hearts may need and respond only to the tender touch of the most meek and gentle channel of My Love, My Healing Power. Now go forth in My Power, to save, to heal, to comfort the brokenhearted."

April 17

So do not fear, for I am with you; do not be dismayed,
for I am your God.
I will strengthen you and help you; I will uphold you with My Righteous Right Hand.
[ISAIAH 41:10]

And my God will meet all your needs according to His Glorious Riches in Christ Jesus.
[PHILIPPIANS 4:19]

May the LORD uphold you, according to each day's needs.
[1 KINGS 8:59]

"No matter what the day brings, I am there with you — upholding you with My Powerful — yet Gentle Hand. When you have exhausted all your own resources, that is when My Hand supplies — often from sources unknown to you, so that all the Glory can be given to your Sole Source of Abundant, Protective Supply. As a loving father provides for the needs of his children, so does your Father — out of My Limitless Supply. Do not fear. I am with you. I will uphold you according to each day's needs. Run to My Awaiting Arms of Love. And as that Supply comes, run on with the word of your testimony of My Loving Supply. Let your life be the proof of My Love."

April 18

*With the tongue we praise our LORD and Father,
and with it we curse men, who have been made
in God's likeness.*
[JAMES 3:9]

I will take refuge in the shadow of Your Wings until the disaster has passed.
[PSALM 57:1b]

Keep me as the apple of Your Eye; hide me in the shadow of Your Wings.
[PSALM 17:8]

"You are Mine. No evil can befall you that is not allowed to train you up in the way you should go — or that is invited in by your own desires, or your own despondency, or your own disobedience, or an unobstructed curse. With My Power, which is readily available to you, tear down, cancel, and destroy those curses; stand strong against those evil attacks you have let in — and destroy their power when I reveal them to you. Follow Me, step by step, and even the rough places can be made smooth and the winding roads be made straight. Walk rightly — go forward — hidden in the shadow of My Wings in safety."

April 19

Find rest, O my soul, in God alone;
my Hope comes from Him.
[PSALM 62:5]

"I love you, child. Feel My Presence and My Tender, Loving, Compassionate Touch on your life. And you will always be at rest in your soul. Come to Me moment by moment and I will give you rest."

April 20

May Your Unfailing Love rest upon us, O LORD.
[PSALM 33:22a]

I sought the LORD, and He answered me;
He delivered me from all my fears.
[PSALM 34:4]

"Let no fears assail you. Stand firm against them. But first, come into My Presence and be enwrapped ~~ be embraced ~~ by My Love. That is truly all you really need ~~ My Love embracing you. My Perfect Love shall then immediately cast out all your fears if you rest ~~ if you trust ~~ in My Unfailing Love for you ~~ My Unfailing Love to be your Sole Source of Provision for whatever need is causing you fear. Do you fully trust My Love to be Unfailing? That is the first question you must ask yourself when those fears assail you. Fear is based on doubt. Fear is based on doubt that I will be your Provider . . . your Healer . . . your Protector . . . your Friend . . . your Security . . . your Sole Source of freedom, fulfillment, worth. . . . Do you fully trust My Love to be Unfailing??"

April 21

Be still before the LORD and
wait patiently before Him.
[PSALM 37:7a]

"My Presence will go with you,
and I will give you rest."
[EXODUS 33:14]

Now the LORD is the Spirit, and where the
Spirit of the LORD is, there is Freedom.
[2 CORINTHIANS 3:17]

"My Voice echoes in the inner chambers of your heart. Listen, and you shall hear My WORDS — which then will set you free from doubt and listlessness, fear and shame. And you shall be filled with such Joy and Zest, and Love, Peace and Rest. Life lived in My Presence is the Life of Freedom I promised. It is for this Freedom that I came to set you free — free from the imprisonment of **self**, of oppression, of darkness. So come, child. Sit in the Stillness in My Presence. Be filled and set free — set free to live life in My Abiding Presence."

April 22

Praise be to the LORD, to God our Savior, Who daily bears our burdens.   Selah
[PSALM 68:19]

"I will never forsake you when you cast your burdens upon Me. When in your desperation, cast your burdens on Me, singing or praying in the Spirit, and I will most surely answer, and release you from your fears, your anguish, your doubt, your desperation. Trust Me fully to answer your prayers, and reward your sacrifice of praise and thanksgiving. My Love, and Care, and Compassion are limitless. Trust Me fully. I will never forsake you, or leave you to carry those burdens alone. You are Mine ~~ Mine to hold in the Palm of My Hand, and nurture, and protect, and love. Trust Me."

April 23

But as for me, I am filled with Power, with the Spirit of the LORD.
[MICAH 3:8a]

"You are filled with My Power when you are filled with My Spirit. Ask for it. Use it. Call on My Power to fill you as never before. . . . Now, release that Power to work in your life — in the lives of those in need — to cancel the work of the enemy. And release that Power to pour out My Blessings — My Favor — My Love, Joy, Peace, Healing, Life — into those lives. Use that Power to bind evil, and to release what is Good into the hearts, the souls, the bodies, the lives, the relationships, the ministries that you lift up to Me. You cannot foresee the Mighty Works that are in store, when you release that Power."

April 24

The LORD longs to be gracious to you.
[ISAIAH 30:18a]

*Now if we are children, then we are heirs —
heirs of God and co-heirs with Christ.*
[ROMANS 8:17a]

*"My son," the father said, "you are always
with me, and everything I have is yours."*
[LUKE 15:31]

Ask and it will be given to you.
[MATTHEW 7:7a]

"You are a child of the King. Do you realize what that means?? Do you realize what that makes you?? That makes you a co-heir with Christ of the Riches of My Kingdom. . . . Unfailing, Limitless Unconditional Love . . . Undisturbed Peace . . . Joy that reaches the depths of your soul . . . a key to My Heavenly Storehouse of Blessings and Favor beyond your imagining. Appropriate those Riches. Ask and you shall receive. Never stop asking — never stop appropriating those riches. They are yours for the asking. Never fail to ask. The King awaits your requests."

April 25

Praise be to the God and Father of our LORD Jesus Christ, the Father of all Compassion and the God of all Comfort, Who comforts us in all our troubles, so that we can comfort those in any trouble with the comfort we ourselves have received from God.
[2 CORINTHIANS 1:3-4]

"Watch for times I can use you to comfort those in sorrow ~~ to care for those in need. Come daily ~~ come moment by moment ~~ into My Presence, to hear how to step out in faith. Fear not. I will be with you, leading and guiding you each step of the way. I have gifted you with the right tools to be My Hands of Mercy and Grace ~~ My Touch of Healing and Love. Trust Me fully. I will provide beyond your imagining. To not trust Me, is like another stripe upon My Back. I love you, child. Trust Me. Do My Bidding."

April 26

Love must be sincere.
Honor one another above yourselves.
[ROMANS 12:9a,10b]

Be imitators of God . . .
and live a life of love, just as Christ loved us
and gave Himself up for us.
[EPHESIANS 5:1-2a]

"Making others' dreams come true ~~ over and above your own ~~ is one of the greatest joys your heart can experience ~~ if you will approach it out of unconditional, selfless, Agape Love. Doing it grudgingly leads only to frustration, un-forgivingness, discontent, anger. . . . But unselfishly fulfilling the needs and desires of others fills your own heart with joy and contentment, even if it means your own hopes and dreams are lost or unfulfilled. That is My Call on your life ~~ to live and love as I did on earth ~~ selflessly giving My ALL ~~ out of My Deep Love for you." Selah

April 27

But He said to me, "My Grace is sufficient for you, for My Power is made perfect in weakness." Therefore, I will boast all the more gladly about my weaknesses, so that Christ's Power may rest on me.
[2 CORINTHIANS 12:9]

"The root of all fears is lack of trust in My Keeping Power — lack of trust that I will come through for you in your times of weakness. I see you doubting your own ability, and viewing that as a weakness, which then causes you fear of how you appear to others. That can be as prideful as thinking too highly of yourself. But when you see your own inability as an avenue for My Strength — My Keeping Power — My Works to be displayed more powerfully in your life — and you find joy in that, then that is evidence of a humble heart. Your lack displays My Abundance — My Merciful, Gracious Provision — when you approach Me with a humble, trusting plea for help, and then go out with joyous praise for My Faithful, Plentiful Provision."

April 28

I call on You, O God, for You will answer me;
give ear to me and hear my prayer. Show the
wonder of Your Great Love.
[PSALM 17:6-7a]

"Child, sit with Me. Rest in My Arms. Tell Me you love Me with your whole heart, and you trust Me fully. You know not the Joy and Comfort and Cheer you bring to Me, as My Presence fills your heart and surrounds you, and fills you with Joy and Peace, Love and Rest. ~~ Mutual Comfort. Think of it, child. Then you will never fail to come near to Me again. I love you, child. Come very near. You will see wonders unfold and displayed. So come."

April 29

Sow for yourselves righteousness, reap the fruit of unfailing love, and break up unplowed ground; for it is time to seek the LORD, until He comes and showers righteousness on you. But you have planted wickedness, you have reaped evil, you have eaten the fruit of deception. Because you have depended on your own strength. . . the roar of battle will rise.
[HOSEA 10:12,13,14a]

"I will work all things together for your good if you will allow Me to — and not rebel, or push against Me, or persist in pursuing your own choices in your own strength. When you turn from your wicked, wayward ways, watch Me work on your behalf. Break up the fallow ground, and plant seeds of righteousness. In due season, you will reap the fruit of Love, Joy, Peace, Bounty. Seek Me — seek My Will — seek My Face. There it is you will reap Unfailing Love. Take My Yoke upon you in this sowing season, and the breaking of the ground and the sowing of the seed will be less burdensome, for My Yoke is easy and My burden is light."

April 30

You were taught, with regard to your former way of life, to put off your old self.
[EPHESIANS 4:22a]

For the waywardness of the simple will kill them, and the complacency of fools will destroy them; but whoever listens to Me will live in safety and be at ease, without fear of harm.
[PROVERBS 1:32-33]

"Child, I long to fill you with My Peace, but first I need you to ask Me to empty you of all past sin — all complacency — and most of all, of self. Only then can you come to Perfect Peace, and know I am holding you close to Me and walking along side you. I am your Protector, your Shield, your Strong Tower. Run to Me and find Strength, Peace, Shelter from the attacks of the enemy and from the strife of tongues. Come to Me and cast every burden on Me. I then can fill you with Peace, and you will find Rest for your weary, troubled soul. So come."

May 1

Seek the LORD while He may be found; call on Him while He is near.
[ISAIAH 55:6]

Keep yourselves in God's Love.
[JUDE 1:21a]

But as for me, it is good to be near God.
[PSALM 73:28]

"My child, this time of intimate fellowship is such a sweet expression of our love for each other. Walking in the Garden with Adam was My Heart's desire as I fashioned him from clay. It was My Heart's desire when I fashioned you in your mother's womb. Come often to this Garden of Love."

May 2

The LORD is Good, a Refuge in times of trouble. He cares for those who trust in Him.
[NAHAM 1:7]

I am the Vine; you are the branches. If a man remains in Me and I in him, he will bear much fruit; apart from Me you can do nothing.
[JOHN 15:5]

Trust in the LORD with all your heart and lean not on your own understanding; in all your ways acknowledge Him, and He will make your paths straight.
[PROVERBS 3:5-6]

"Yes, child, I do make all the circumstances in your life work together for your ultimate good, or that of someone you love. It may not seem that way, as you go through the trials or the pain, but you cannot see the mosaic each step of the way. As you willingly submit to My Will, and make My Will your will, wait for My Work to be displayed in your life. Lay down your selfish will — for My Will — for Me — for My Purposes. Choose My Ways, and watch for the fruit to come forth — fruit you never would have known to ask for, or to expect to come forth from your life. Trust Me with your life. You will see wonders unfold."

May 3

Now the LORD is the Spirit, and where the Spirit of the LORD is, there is freedom. And we, who with unveiled faces all reflect the LORD's Glory, are being transformed into His likeness with ever-increasing Glory, which comes from the LORD, Who is the Spirit.
[2 CORINTHIANS 3:17-18]

"At times I must strip you of your own power, so you will operate totally under — and with — My Power. Listen — speak out. Listen — reach out. Discern — walk in faith. . . . You need not be perfect. — You need not be whole. — You need not be never wrong. — You need not have every tool, every talent, every ability, to be used by Me. My Power is made Perfect in your weaknesses. When you are in your most humble state, then My Glory will shine Brightest. — My Power will be what is displayed — not yours. Let Me be God. — Let Me do the work. — Let Me shine forth My Light in the darkness. You are My lamp to shine forth My Light into the dark places where I am sending you. Be led — be fed — be used by My Power, by My Spirit within you. Go in Peace. Go in Power. Go forth with a humble heart, and be used to lead the lonely, the broken, the lost, to Me."

May 4

Sing to Him, sing praise to Him, tell of all His Wonderful Acts.
[1 CHRONICLES 16:9]

"I have desired from the beginning of time for My people to be worshippers. You were created to worship Me ~~ to bring Me praise, and honor and glory, and to tell of all My Gracious, Loving, Caring, Gentle, Awesome Acts of Kindness, Justice, Love. Use your voice to bring Me praise; live your life to bring Me praise."

May 5

How great are Your Works, O LORD, how profound Your Thoughts!
[PSALM 92:5]

"It brings Joy to My Heart when you find delight in Me ~~ in My Works ~~ in My Thoughts. Dear friends find delight in each other's thoughts and actions, when they have deep devotion and love for each other. Draw closer and closer to Me ~~ in oneness ~~ as our friendship deepens. . . . And as our friendship deepens, you will know Me ~~ truly know Me ~~ My Thoughts ~~ My Character ~~ My Nature ~~ My Love. . . . Be captured by My Love. . . . You will be changed."

May 6

I keep asking that the God of our LORD Jesus
Christ, the Glorious Father, may give you the
Spirit of Wisdom and Revelation, so that you
may know Him better.
I pray also that the eyes of your heart may
be enlightened
in order that you may know the Hope to
which He has called you, the Riches of His
Glorious Inheritance in the saints, and
His incomparably Great Power for us who
believe. That Power is like the working of
His Mighty Strength, which He exerted in
Christ when He raised Him from the dead
and seated Him in the heavenly realms, far
above all rule and authority, power and
dominion, and every title that can be given,
not only in the present age
but also in the one to come

[EPHESIANS 1:17-21]

"My Mercy, My Grace and Goodness, My Loving-Kindnesses are ever-available. And because you are My child, you are My Heir to these Riches — these Treasures. These are the Riches of your Glorious Inheritance — to be received even now. You are living your eternal kingdom life right now. And your Inheritance is ever-available. Learn to appropriate it. Claim it. Walk in it. When stress assails you, claim My Mercy, My Grace and Goodness, to ease your soul. When under attack, listen not to the lies of the enemy. Claim My

Loving-Kindness to surround you. Appropriate My Great Power to strike down the enemy and send him fleeing."

May 7

"My sheep listen to My Voice; I know them, and they follow Me.
[JOHN 10:27]

Commit thy way unto the LORD; trust in Him also; and He shall bring it to pass.
[PSALM 37:5 (KJV)]

"Are you one of My sheep who hear My Voice, and follow Me? If so, never fear. I will lead you and guide you along the path I have for you. When you are truly committed to making your way, My Way — your will, My Will — I shall bring it to pass, since you have given up all rights to your own way — your own will — your **self**. When you truly commit your way to Me, and you humbly embrace Me, My Love will thrill you, comfort you, surround you, fill you — thrill you. Commit your way to Me — become one with Me — and you will know that I am for you, not against you. I am your sole Provider. Trust in Me, and I shall bring it to pass."

May 8

Just as He Who called you is Holy, so be Holy in all you do; for it is written: "Be Holy, because I am Holy."
[1 PETER 1:15 / LEVITICUS 11:44,45; 19:2; 20:7,26]

[God disciplines His Sons]
Let us throw off everything that hinders and the sin that so easily entangles, and let us run with perseverance the race marked out for us.
[HEBREWS 12:1b]

"Holy — Holy is My Nature. And that is My ultimate goal for you. Run for that goal. And as you run that race set before you, take time to sit in My Presence and take in the Refreshment of My WORD — the Bread of Life . . .and the Refreshment of My Living Water. — Let My Spirit wash over you — refreshing you and re-energizing you to run the next lap. Each lap will bring its own new challenges . . . and joys. You will need My Refreshing Bread and Water to feed you and wash over you daily. When a lap is intensely draining, you need My Refreshing Water — moment by moment — to stay in the race. Left out on your own, your strength fades quickly."

May 9

The LORD is near to all who call upon Him, to all who call upon Him sincerely and in truth.
[PSALM 145:18 (AMP)]

"Being in constant communion with Me is your Source of Strength, and Hope, and Direction. You will know My Truth — My Truth for each moment, each movement. But fear will prevent you from walking in My Way for you. Fear is the enemy's way of immobilizing you — and keeping you from being used for My Glory. Fight fear. Come near Me. Listen only to My Voice of Truth, and become the victor. Change fear to faith — by speaking My WORD over you — over each step. Give your life — give your moments — to Me, and I will use you to the full. Step by step I will use you — I will lead you to walk in My Ways, to do Mighty Works — Tender Works — Loving Works — in My Name — for My Glory."

May 10

Let us draw near to God with a sincere heart in full assurance of faith, having our hearts sprinkled to cleanse us from a guilty conscience.
[HEBREWS 10:22]

"Come into My Presence with thanksgiving in your heart, having laid your burdens at My Feet. Confess now, and lay your guilt at My Feet. Be set free to worship Me with all your heart. I wash you with My Blood — through and through — no stain remains. You are forgiven and fully cleansed. Walk in newness of life. — Walk humbly before Me. — Walk under the Shelter of My Wings. — Walk nearer and nearer to Me each day. Be set free to love Me — to serve Me — to serve Me and worship Me with all your heart. I love you, child. Be set free."

May 11

The LORD longs to be gracious to you;
He rises to show you compassion.
[PSALM 30:18a]

The Faithful Love of the LORD never ends!
His Mercies never cease.
[LAMENTATIONS 3:22(NLT)]

"I love you, child. Feel My Presence . . . My Tender, Loving, Compassionate Touch on your life ~~ on your heart. And you will always be at rest in your soul. Come to Me ~~ moment by moment ~~ come to Me. And I will give you rest ~~ embraced by My Presence ~~ embraced by My Love."

May 12

*He performs wonders that cannot be
fathomed,
miracles that cannot be counted.*
[JOB 5:9; 9:10]

*You are the God Who performs miracles;
You display Your Power among the peoples.*
[PSALM 77:14]

"I give you many miracles that you so often fail to recognize. . . . A wound that heals so quickly . . . a car that
barely misses your bumper . . . a light that turns red to
delay you long enough to miss the vehicle that runs the
next red light . . . your child comes home safely . . . your
spouse hears My Gentle Whisper to give you a call just
when you needed them . . . your spouse hears and obeys
My Command to forgive you — to not get angry — to
come home on time — to be faithful to their promise. . . .
All things done through the outpouring of My Power—
impossible in mere human power in those moments —
but natural outpourings of My Supernatural Power and
Love — — daily Miracles. Watch for them. — Then Love,
Joy, revelation will fill your heart, and praise will be on
your lips."

May 13

You need to persevere so that when you have done the Will of God, you will receive what He has promised.
[HEBREWS 10:36]

"Persevere when all seems lost — and I will step in with My Redeeming Power, and bring all things together for your good. You will gain Strength when you lean back on My Strong Arms — on My Enduring Love. . . . My Love will fill you, enwrap you, strengthen you, encourage you, empower you. . . . Persevere when all seems lost, and you will see My Power at work, when you lean back — in trust — into My Loving Arms. I will not fail you, when you lean not on your own understanding, but lean on Me — in faith — out of a pure, humble heart — admitting your own lack — and depending on Me alone. — Find My Rest for your weary soul — and Peace, and Joy — when you recognize My Hand holding you — My Loving Arms embracing you — My Redeeming Power at work in your life."

May 14

I will praise You, O LORD, with all my heart;
I will tell of all Your Wonders.
I will be glad and rejoice in You;
I will sing praise
to Your Name, O Most High.
[PSALM 9:1,2]

I trust in Your Unfailing Love;
my heart rejoices in Your Salvation.
[PSALM 13:5]

Then the man bowed low and
worshiped the LORD.
[GENESIS 24:26(NASB)]

Do you see what we've got?
An unshakable kingdom!
And do you see how thankful we must be?
Not only thankful, but brimming with
worship,
deeply reverent before God.
[HEBREWS 12:28(MSG)]

"Worship must be a tender expression of a thankful heart — or a shout of praise out of a joyful heart — or a sweet expression of a heart of love reflecting on My Goodness . . . My Grace . . . My Mercy . . . My Healing . . . My Provision . . . My Unconditional Unfailing Unending Love — or a longing look at My Face — or a stream of tears from being in My Presence. — No matter the form of your worship, the Father looks only at the depths of your heart."

May 15

The LORD delights in those who fear Him, who put their hope in His Unfailing Love.
[PSALM 147:11]

"You are Mine. And when you come to Me like this, it melds us together in perfect unity. Stay close to Me. That fills My Heart with Joy when My children come to Me ~~ just to be with Me. ~~ Not in supplication. ~~ Not even in confession and repentance. But the coming away with Me to this Secret Place ~~ that is what gives Me Joy. Think ~~ ponder ~~ that you bring Joy to the Master and Creator of this vast universe just by drawing near to Me ~~ just to be with Me ~~ in union with Me. So come. Remain in Me and I will remain with you ~~ in you. Keep this time pure. Set yourself apart for Me. Come away with Me. Let Me pour out My Love, My Hope, My Peace, My Purity into your heart ~~ into your spirit ~~ and pour out My Healing Power over you and through you. Drink from My Well of Life ~~ My Living Water. Take My Hand, and follow Me into this Secret Place."

May 16

"This is the meaning of the parable: The seed is the WORD of God. The seed on good soil stands for those with a noble and good heart, who hear the WORD, retain it, and by persevering produce a crop, a hundred times more than was sown."
[LUKE 8:11,15,8b]

The fruit of the Spirit is love, joy, peace, patience, kindness, goodness, faithful, gentleness and self-control.
[GALATIANS 5:22]

"There is still much to do to till up the fallow ground of your heart, where no fruit is found growing. But as you yield your heart, your self to My Hand, the fruit produced is a sweet fragrance to Me. I am at work in your life. But there is still much to do to produce the continual harvest of fragrant fruit. Keep the soil well-watered with My Spirit, well-fertilized with your prayers during these times of sweet oneness in My Inner Courts. And let Me plant the Seeds of My WORD meant just for your fertile heart. Together we will take joy in the abundant harvest."

May 17

Therefore, as God's chosen people, holy and dearly loved, clothe yourselves with compassion, kindness, humility, gentleness and patience.
[COLOSSIANS 3:12]

I desire to do Your Will, O my God; Your law is within my heart.
[PSALM 40:8]

O God, You are my God, earnestly I seek You; my soul thirsts for You, my body longs for You.
[PSALM 63:1]

"Child, make Me your one desire in life — knowing Me . . . loving Me . . . following Me . . . becoming one with Me . . . serving Me . . . sharing My Life and My Love with others . . . showing compassion — My Compassion — to the hurting and the needy . . . setting the captives free with your prayers and My Love. Make Me the driving desire in your life."

May 18

The LORD your God is with you, He is Mighty to save.
He will take great delight in you,
He will quiet you with His Love.
[ZEPHANIAH 3:17]

"You are My precious child. I love you more than you can ever know. Rest. Rest in My Loving Arms. Renew your strength. These times alone with Me shall renew your strength. . . . These times alone with Me must reassure you of your worth to Me. Come away with Me into these times of quiet communion . . . and wait. . . . Wait until you are sure of My Love . . . My Tender Love. . . . Rest now . . . in My Quieting Love."

May 19

I made you grow like a plant of the field.
You grew up and developed and became the
most beautiful of jewels.
[EZEKIEL 16:7a]

I thank my God every time I remember you.
In all my prayers for you, I always pray with
joy because of your partnership in the Gospel
from the first day until now.
It is right for me to feel this way about you,
since I have you in my heart.
[PHILIPPIANS 1:3-5,7a]

"When you make a difference in the lives of others, that is when you see yourself as having worth. You have worth to them. — You have worth to Me. — And that is what gives you worth in your own eyes — a deep-down sense of worth. Your value comes directly from Me. When those in the world value you — is it for the right reasons? Do they see the treasure inside you? Do they love you because of the treasure I've placed inside you? Reflect My Kingdom — be the essence of My Love — and they cannot help but be drawn to you. Those who truly value Me, will value you — if you truly, deeply value Me — in full measure. Consecrate your life to Me. And My sensitive-hearted people will keep you in their hearts, because of your dedication to Me. And their love for you will then give you a deep sense of worth in My Kingdom."

May 20

For the king trusts in the LORD; through the
Unfailing Love of the Most
High he will not be shaken.
[PSALM 21:7]

Then they cried out to the LORD in their
trouble.
He stilled the storm to a whisper; the waves of
the sea were hushed!
[PSALM 107:28a,29]

"When all around rises into chaos, My people have various responses . . . fear, rage, deep-seated anger, withdrawal, rebellion, retaliation, weariness, anxiety, despair, indignation. . . . But My desire for you is trust, patience, wisdom, and most of all prayer — fervent prayer — faithfully calling upon My Power to be released. It is by My Hand, My WORD, My Power that calms the raging sea. It is your prayers, your trust — your release of those burdens — that sets My Power in motion."

May 21

Turn my heart toward Your Statutes and not toward selfish gain.
[PSALM 119:36]

"Self is such a drainer of Life — drainer of My Agape Love — My Unconditional, self-less Love. When you choose self over Me, and you pursue self-satisfaction and self-ish pleasures, you reject My Love — My Provision — My Blessings — My WORD. Do not ignore Me! — What Eternal Blessings you miss out on, when you ignore Me! I am your Redeemer — your Friend. I laid My Life down for you. What greater gift is there? Lay your life down — your self down at My Feet. And be lifted up to greater Blessings — deeper Love — greater Heights than you have ever known."

May 22

[Making One's Calling and Election Sure]
His Divine Power has given us everything
we need for life and godliness through our
knowledge of Him Who called us by His Own
Glory
and Goodness.
[2 PETER 1:3]

O Sovereign LORD, You are God! Your Words
are Trustworthy, and You have promised
these things
to Your servant.
[2 SAMUEL 7:28]

"Trust Me with Your very life. I long to give you life — My Life — the life that I've planned for you, full of favor and godliness and Truth — and freedom from sin and this world's grip on you. Many lessons are required along the way to prepare the way, and to prepare you for walking that path with Me. Trust Me fully. Walk with Me. Give Me your hand. Give Me your trust. Give Me your love. Give Me the gift of the moments — all the moments. Then watch Me do Mighty Miracles in your life — with your life — in your heart."

May 23

*I have seen You in the sanctuary and beheld
Your Power and Glory.*
[PSALM 63:2]

*No eye has seen, no ear has heard,
no mind has conceived what God has
prepared
for those who love Him — but God has
revealed
it to us by His Spirit.
The Spirit searches all things, even the deep
things of God.*
[1 CORINTHIANS 2:9-10]

"Go forward fearlessly. When you allow fear to rule your
heart — to rule your thoughts — to rule your actions,
your responses, your mood — you lose sight of My Hand
at work in your life. You lose sight of My Loving Arms
enfolding you — supporting you in the flight. Soar on
My Wings. Let Me carry you through the flight. Trust
Me to take you to new heights you have yet not known.
There is so much more to My Kingdom that you have yet
to experience. Knowing about Me is not truly knowledge
of Me, until you experience My Power at work. Take My
Hand. I will lead you to the Land of Plenty — where My
Kingdom is on display. Watch, and wait. Wait until My
Power is released among the people. Appropriate that
Power — use My Power as I prompt you. Wait for My Still
Small Voice to prompt you. You will know by My Peace,
that it is My Voice of Truth, prompting you into action.

Be My Touch of Healing. Be My Touch of Tenderness. Be My Touch of Loving Kindness. Be My Touch of Peace and Freedom. . . . Wait, and watch for My Power to be displayed among you. When the Impartation of My Spirit is experienced, fear can no longer rule you. When the Impartation of My Spirit is experienced, you begin to know Who I really am."

May 24

Who is like You ~~ Majestic in Holiness,
Awesome in Glory, working wonders?
[EXODUS 15:11]

Come near to God and He will come near to
you.
[JAMES 4:8]

"Stand in awe of My Majesty. Look into My Face. Draw nearer ~~ ever nearer ~~ into My Very Presence. I am with you ~~ I am in you. I surround you ~~ I fill you ~~ with My Presence . . . My Love . . . My Compassion. . . . Come nearer ~~ ever nearer ~~ each time you come to Me to seek My Touch."

May 25

I have seen your tears and heard all your prayers. I will heal you.
[2 KINGS 20:5b]

I will give You thanks, for You answered me.
[PSALM 118:21b]

"I have seen all your tears, and hear all your prayers. I will heal your broken heart ~~ as you release your fears . . . your cares . . . your woes . . . to Me. ~~ I will gather you into My Arms and carry you close to My Heart as you mourn your loss. You will know the healing has begun when you can turn to Me with a thankful heart. Pour out your heart to Me. ~~ ~~ Soon, every tear shed will come from a thankful heart for My Tender Touch . . . for My Love . . . for My Forgiveness . . . for My Love . . . My Peace . . . My Love."

May 26

Show me Your Ways, O LORD,
teach me Your Paths;
guide me in Your Truth and teach me, for
You are my Savior, and my hope is in You,
all the day long.
[PSALM 25:4-5]

"When self fills your being, you have no room for Me. . . . You have no time for Me. . . . You think you have no need of Me — no need of Me with the little day-to-day happenings — but only with the big, heavy pressures on your life. I must bring you first to repentance — for the distance you have put between us. . . . Now, draw near to Me — not just for the heavy burdens to be lifted — yes, do that— but, also, for the moments of need . . . the moments of praise . . . the moments of fear . . . the moments of panic . . . the moments of joy . . . the moments of anguish . . . the moments of loving trust . . . the moments of thankful praise . . . the moments of need. I love you, child. Draw near to Me. Trust Me. Give Me your moments."

May 27

I pray also that the eyes of your heart may be enlightened in order that you may know the hope to which He has called you, the riches of His glorious inheritance in the saints, and His incomparably great Power for us who believe.
[EPHESIANS 1:18-19a]

"Step into My Kingdom — your Inheritance. . . . You are a child of the King of kings — heir to the Abundance of My Kingdom. Claim your Inheritance — appropriate your supply. Then bend down in honor of the King. Then come, child, come very near. Come into My Inner Chamber. Wait expectantly in My Holy of Holies. . . . You will never be the same."

May 28

Let us then approach the Throne of Grace with confidence, so that we may receive mercy and find grace to help us in our time of need.
[HEBREWS 4:16]

"Precious child, hear My Voice — My Voice alone. Let not the darkness overtake you. Come running to Me in every time of need — physical pain . . . mental anguish . . . broken heart . . . fear overshadowing you . . . doubt . . . unrest . . . failure . . . loneliness . . . sorrow . . . sadness. . . . — In everything, seek Me first, and I will give you Rest and Care, Love and Joy, Peace and Faith — all out of My Kingdom Supply. . . . My Heart . . . My Power . . . My Love . . . My Strength — My Kingdom Supply."

May 29

I cry out to God Most High, to God, Who fulfills His purpose for me.
[PSALM 57:2]

"Child, you are precious to Me. I created you for a purpose. You are beginning to fulfill that purpose — even as you stumble. Seek Me — not only first — but all throughout your day. And I will set you free from strife, from bondage, from enemy attacks, free from fear, from your pain of your breaking heart. You are precious to Me. Seek Me, as you would your dearest friend."

May 30

Commit your way to the LORD; trust in Him
and
He will do this:
He will make your righteousness
shine like the dawn.
[PSALM 37:5,6]

"Stay by My Side, dear child, watching and waiting for Your Shepherd to lead you along still waters — or raging streams . . . beside green pastures — or in the wilderness of temptation. . . . The tempting — as Mine was — is a mark of true discipleship — first to test your devotion to Me — your trust in Me. . . . And 2nd, to teach you to stand firm against the enemy. Either way, it is the road to maturity in your growing likeness to Me."

May 31

*Be still before the LORD and
wait patiently for Him.*
[PSALM 37:7a]

*But as for me, I watch in hope for the LORD,
I wait for God my Savior.*
[MICAH 7:7]

*How great is Your Goodness, which You have
stored up for those who fear You, which You
bestow in the sight of men on those who take
refuge in You.*
[PSALM 31:19]

"I will use you for My Glory when you put yourself in My Hands. Wait, child — wait on My Goodness to do immeasurably more than you could ever ask or imagine. Wait before Me — yielded and still. Then, it is, that I can mold you into a pure vessel — to be filled with My Spirit. Let Me use you according to My Good Pleasure — and I will show the world My Miracle-Working Power — that can be used in their lives — if only they would come to Me, yielded and still. Listen for My Voice calling you into action. . . . But first, wait. . . . Just wait. . . . Wait for My Love — My Spirit — to fill you and ready you for action."

June 1

O LORD my God, You are very great; You are
clothed with splendor and majesty. . . .
He stretches out the heavens like a tent. . . .
He makes springs pour water into the
ravines. . . . The birds of the air nest by the
waters, they sing among the branches. . . .
The earth is satisfied by the fruit of His
Work. . . . He makes grass grow for the
cattle. . . . The trees of the LORD are well
watered. . . . There the birds make their
nest. . . .
The moon marks off the seasons, and the sun
knows when to go down. . . .
How many are Your Works, O LORD! In
Wisdom
You made them all; the earth is full
of Your creatures.
. . . I will sing to the LORD all my life; I will
sing praise to my God as long as I live.
[PSALM 104:1,2,10,12,13,14,16,17,19,24,33]

"When you come to Me as a little child — finding delight in just being out in My creation with your Abba Father— not only your spirit and weary soul are being made whole, but your body is being nurtured and healed and energized. — Alive in My Spirit — made alive by Your Creator constantly creating you into a new creature, more and more reflecting My Image. I created you — and still am creating you — in My Image. Dwell much with Me out here in My creation, soaking in My Love and My Beauty.

Live much with Me in My creation. As Adam and Eve did in the Garden of Eden, walk with Me in My gardens, and you yourself will be a lovely flowering fruit-producing creation, taking on My Image. I am Love. Bear the Fruit of Love. — Above all — bear the Fruit of Love. Live much with Me and you will overflow with My Love. So come, and walk with Me in My Gardens."

June 2

"Even now," declares the LORD, *"return to Me with all your heart, with fasting, and weeping, and mourning."*
[JOEL 2:12]

I have swept away your offenses like a cloud, your sins like the morning mist. Return to Me, for I have redeemed you.
[ISAIAH 44:22]

"Come, follow Me," Jesus said, "and I will make you fishers of men."
[MARK 1:17]

"My WORD to you, My people, has been the same throughout the ages: 'COME, FOLLOW ME!' 'RETURN TO ME!' 'WALK WITH ME.' I love you, child, and I want you near Me."

"COME FOLLOW ME."

June 3

Today, if you hear His Voice,
do not harden your heart.
[PSALM 95:8a]

I will listen to what God the LORD will say;
He promises peace to His people.
[PSALM 85:8a]

Those who hope in the LORD
will renew their strength.
They will soar on wings like eagles.
[ISAIAH 40:31a]

"Hear My Voice, child. Hear My Voice calling you to rise on My Wings, and soar like an eagle on the Wind of My Spirit, rising higher and higher, in My Divine Strength. A hardened heart will cause you to stumble, and fall away from Me — from My Peace — My Provision — My Safety. But a heart seeking after Me will be given Peace and Security — and will soar with Me on the Wind of My Spirit, rising higher and higher, in My Divine Strength."

June 4

*It is God who arms me with strength and
makes my way perfect.
He makes my feet like the feet of a deer;
He enables me to stand on the heights.*
[2 SAMUEL 22:33-34]

"Come, child. I gently lead you on the straight path. When you stumble and fall, I reach down to pick you up to continue the race. Do not allow the enemy to accuse you over and over. I have set you free to run the race with Me. Feel My Arms around you — supporting you, comforting you, washing you clean, healing your wounds, erasing the scars of past failures. Run away with Me. Seek Freedom from the enemy attacks. Come into My Inner Chambers and be set free from the lies and attacks of the enemy. Seek shelter in My Loving Presence — where no evil can stand."

June 5

Love the LORD your God and walk in all His ways and keep His commandments and hold fast to Him and serve Him with all your heart and with all your soul.
[JOSHUA 22:5b (NAS)]

I long to dwell in Your tent forever and take refuge in the shelter of Your Wings. Selah
[PSALM 61:4]

My soul yearns for You in the night; in the morning my spirit longs for You.
[ISAIAH 26:9]

For great is Your Love toward me.
[PSALM 86:13a]

"Live in Me. ~~ Nurtured by My Love. ~~ Calm and secure in My Arms. Love Me with your whole heart. Live in My Presence daily ~~ moment by moment. Carry your burdens to My Feet. Drop them there ~~ never to be picked up again. Listen and learn of My Ways for your life. Hear My Voice amid the voices of this world that speak and hold your attention. Listen to My Voice above all others. Listen. Learn. Grow in My Ways as you walk by My Side throughout your day. ~~ Secure in My Arms. ~~ Safe from harm. ~~ Sheltered from the enemy's attacks. Come close. Keep close to Me and you will long for Me more and more. ~~ Energized by My Love . . . My Presence . . . My Sheltering Arms . . . My Voice . . . My Love. Be free. Be loved. Be held. Be Mine."

June 6

But you, when you pray, go into your room,
and when you have shut the door,
pray to your Father Who is in the Secret Place;
and your Father Who sees in secret
will reward you openly.
[MATTHEW 6:6 (NKJV)]

"You do not have to be in our Secret Place to hear My Whispers, though the intimacy of our Secret Place fulfills your desire — your need — for time alone with Me, when your spirit intermingles with My Loving Spirit, and you are immersed in My Presence. But you can hear My Whispers even in a crowd. It only takes a listening ear, and an open heart, and a trained, willing spirit to hear My Voice. It is in our Secret Place where that training occurs. The more time you spend with Me in our Secret Place, the more you learn to clearly discern My Voice, and find rest and peace for your soul. Listen to My Voice and live in harmony with My Guidance. And you will see marvels unfold before you. Do not underestimate the influence you can have — the influence you do have on others, as you hear My Whispers and follow My Guidance. Seek Me first — seek first to hear and follow My Still, Small Voice. — And all else will be provided. Go in Peace."

June 7

Then you will call to Me and come and pray to Me, and I will listen to you. You will seek Me and find Me when you seek Me with all your heart.
[JEREMIAH 29:12-13]

"My child, your need is My call. I await your prayers, which tear down the barriers you have put around you, that keep you from Me. Acknowledge your needs to Me. Call them by name — honestly — from your heart. Confession may need to accompany your prayers, to unblock the barriers. Come humbly to Me — not begging or pleading as to someone who is reluctant to give you aid. — But to your Dearest Friend, Your Ever-Loving Father. Sometimes the answers to your prayers must be, 'No,' to protect you or someone you love. Join hands with Me, and know My Love is at work for your good. Trust Me. Know that I am He Who sees all your needs, and meets those needs in generous supply."

June 8

As the Father loved Me, I also have loved you;
abide in My love.
[JOHN 15:9 (NKJV)]

"Listen and you will hear the secrets of heaven spoken to your very ear. Abide in My Love ~~ My Sheltering Arms. Draw close ~~ in worship, in prayer ~~ in life. Abide. Abide in My Love ~~ My Sheltering Arms. Abide."

June 9

I cry to You for help, O LORD, every day; I spread out my hands to You. I cry to You for help, O LORD; in the morning my prayer comes before You.
[PSALM 89:9,13]

"Supply will come for every work I ask of you. Be sure of it. — Walk in it. Live in My Presence and know that I AM. I am your Supplier, Deliverer, Dearest Friend. . . .

-Supplier for your every need — not every want — but your every true need

-Deliverer — from self — from attacks of the enemy when you walk in My Path and call on My Power to deliver you

-Dearest Friend — so Intimate, so Divine, so Reassuring, so Loving and Kind, Deepest Listener of your every thought — your every word, Constant Companion. . . . Rest in that thought."

June 10

How precious is Your lovingkindness, O God!
How priceless is Your unfailing Love!
[PSALM 36:7a (NASB)/(NIV)]

"I see you through the Eyes of Love. Yes, your human nature is frail and faulty. But covered and washed clean by My Blood, you are a treasure. Remember that Truth when you feel like a failure. — Worthless in your own eyes. . . . A treasure in Mine."

June 11

Your Presence fills me with joy and brings me pleasure forever.
[PSALM 16:11b (GNT)]

"Until you experience My Manifest Presence, you cannot really know Me. In the atmosphere of tender worship melodies, sit back, or bow down, and feel the Manifest Presence of My Spirit enfolding you in My Love ~~ My Peace ~~ My Tender Touch ~~ My Powerful Embrace ~~ My Love. Knowing about Me is only information until you experience My Manifest Presence and Power. ~~ Only then can you know My Heart, My Thoughts, My Desires for you ~~ the depths of My Love for you. Come into My Presence in the stillness, as your thoughts are being totally focused on My Presence ~~ on My Love."

June 12

Take My Yoke upon you and learn from Me,
for I am Gentle and Humble in Heart,
and you will find rest for your soul.
For My Yoke is easy and My burden is light.
[MATTHEW 11:29-30]

Turn my eyes from worthless things;
preserve my life according to Your Word.
[PSALM 119:37]

"Take My Yoke upon you and I will give you the rest that you so desire. My Yoke is easy, making your burden light — when you walk in step with Me — not pulling ahead or lagging behind. I know it is in your heart to be in unity with Me. But your flesh is weak. Come to Me, and I will give you Strength to stand strong against the enemy's attack on your flesh. Your heart's desire is obedience . . . and trust . . . and full submission. — That is precious to Me even when your weaknesses prevent that. Each step you make toward My Perfection draws you closer to Me. There is now no condemnation. Do not listen to condemnation. Listen to My Healing Words . . . My Words of Life . . . My Words of Love."

June 13

As it is written: "There is no one righteous, not even one. All have turned away; they have together become worthless; there is no one who does good, not even one."
[ROMANS 3:10,12]

"In My Eyes you are never worthless when you seek My Will. When you seek My Will, you are My treasure. Then it is, that I can use you to the fullest. I am the Creator of the Universe. And yet, I am the Creator of Mercy — of Saving Grace — of Life Everlasting — of Joy and Love. Under the old law, there was none righteous, not even one. But I came to fulfill the law, and declare you righteous when you seek Me — when you seek My Mercy, My Grace, and My Cleansing Blood and Forgiveness. It is by My Work that makes you righteous — and therefore, never worthless."

June 14

Those who hope in the LORD
will renew their strength.
They will soar on wings like eagles.
[ISAIAH 40:31]

We rejoice in our sufferings, because we
know that suffering produces perseverance;
perseverance, character; and character
hope.
And hope does not disappoint us, because
God has poured out His Love into our hearts
by the Holy Spirit, Whom He has given us.
[ROMANS 5:3-5]

"As you walk through the desert in pain and suffering, My Joy may seem unreachable. But take courage. My Hand will strengthen you, and you will fly on wings like eagles. — Soaring to greater heights than you have ever experienced — as you nestle into My Arms of Love, and know that our Loving Friendship is being deepened and strengthened. Then My Joy will flood your heart, and overflow onto others as you serve Me quietly. I will fill your heart with songs of deliverance, which too, will fill you with Joy. Walk, knowing the best is yet to come."

June 15

Grasp how wide and long and deep is the
Love of Christ — that you may be filled to the
measure of all the Fullness of God.
[EPHESIANS 3:18b,19b]

"Spend your days with Me — embraced by My Love — then all else becomes but a shadow. When you open your heart to the full Embrace of My Love — you will be changed. Suddenly, you will witness Wonders in your midst, since you will recognize My Touch. So much of the world is blind to My Touch. — So many of My people are blind to My Touch — and missing the Joy of My Embrace. Lean now, into My Embrace . . . totally abandoned to Me. . . . No greater Joy. . . . No greater Peace."

June 16

*You are my King and my God. You give us victory
over our enemies.*
[PSALM 44:4a,7a]

With God we will gain the victory.
[PSALM 60:12a; 108:13a]

*'Not by might, nor by power, but by My Spirit,'
says the LORD Almighty.*
[ZECHARIAH 4:6b]

"The world may deem you as a failure. The enemy may say, 'You are a failure. You can't . . .' But I say, 'Go, child. Go and be lifted up on the Wings of My Spirit to soar with Me.' — Then My Victory will be your victory. Your successes will be accomplished through My Spirit — done for Me — by My Spirit working through you. Now walk in My Peace and My Joy into every relationship, every task I lead you to. Go in Peace on the Wings of My Spirit — and conquer. My Victory is yours."

June 17

But as for me, I am filled with Power,
with the Spirit of the LORD.
[MICAH 3:8a]

"When pain attacks your body — your heart — your life — draw close to Me. Pain is sometimes needed to draw you close — ever closer — to Me. NO! I do not cause the pain!! But, yes, I must at times allow the pain — to draw you to your knees to seek Me first. Then I will reveal — to your listening, softened heart — the message you so desperately need to hear. It may be a plucking, a pruning — to reveal the deeper beauty within you. But, oh, it may be a call to battle. Rise! And claim My Power to strike down the enemy. You are Mine. No foe can oppose you that is stronger than I. I am the Victor. The pain — the alert — the call to battle — is not a lack on My part to strike down the enemy. — But a call to train you for the battles. Claim My Power! Declare aloud, 'I am filled with Power with the Spirit of the Living God! And with that Power, I strike down the enemy!!' Come against the enemy, fully equipped for this battle. With Me, you will gain the victory as this facet of the training is completed."

June 18

And now, what does the LORD
your God ask of you
but to fear the LORD your God, to walk in all
His Ways, to love Him, to serve the LORD your
God with all your heart and with all your
soul.
[DEUTERONOMY 10:12]

"I know your heart's desire is to serve Me and honor Me. Your strength, though, may hinder you from doing as many acts of service for Me as you desire right now. But worship and honor comes from a grateful heart. Each time you look My way and say, 'Thank You, LORD,' is an act of worship that honors Me when it comes from deep within your heart. You serve Me in ways you cannot even know right now. Trust Me. Trust Me to bring it to fruition."

June 19

*O, L**ORD**, You are our Father.
We are the clay, You are the Potter;
we are all the work of Your Hand.*
[ISAIAH 64:8]

"Hear Me, child, and be ready to walk according to My Will for you. You will be changed — molded — sometimes stretched — but always held in the Potter's Hands."

June 20

My heart and my flesh cry out for the Living God.
[PSALM 84:2a]

"Seek after Me and My Heavenly Treasures. Set your mind on things above. I hear the cry of your heart to know Me, to hear My Voice. Give Me your moments. Cry out for Me at every turn. Drop your burdens, and fill your heart and thoughts with My Treasures. — Moment by moment I am here for you — waiting to release you of your cares — and fill you with My Presence, My Treasures. Come now. . . . Give Me your moments."

June 21

*In the last days, God says, I will pour out
My Spirit on all people.
Your sons and daughters will prophesy,
your young men will see visions,
your old men will dream dreams.
Even on My servants, both men and women,
I will pour out My Spirit in those days,
and they will prophesy.*
[JOEL 2:28-29; ACTS 2:17-18]

*For the wedding of the Lamb has come,
and His bride has made herself ready.*
[REVELATION 19:7b]

"My Hand is not shortened by any power in this world —
except the power of self. When self takes first place, My
Power is shut out. Also, lack of vision — and fear of the
unknown — greatly block My Miracle-Working Power. It is
only in the open heart, and the spirit longing for My Touch,
that My Power can be released in Full Measure. My Church
at large should be experiencing the Impartation of My Spirit
and the resulting Miracles — as are little pockets of those
seeking Me in Full Measure. But lack of knowledge, lack of
exposure, lack of vision, lack of souls on fire and open to the
Workings of My Spirit prevent My tentrance. I will not force
My Miracle Touch on anyone. You must open the door and
let My Presence fill the atmosphere of your gathering. Then
you must claim My Power for yourself — your heart — your
inner-most being. Just watching it at work in others — with
doubt — with fear in your heart, blocks My entrance into
your heart. An open heart, a spirit longing for more and more
of Me, opens the Way for My Spirit to be released within you.
Pray for that impartation — for yourself first — and then for
My Body at large. I long for My Bride to be readied."

June 22

But as for me, it is good to be near God.
I have made the Sovereign LORD my refuge;
I will tell of all Your Deeds.
[PSALM 73:28]

"When you need Me ~~ when you need My Love ~~ My Sheltering Arms, draw close, and be still ~~ until you sense My Very Presence surrounding you, encompassing you, holding you, washing you with My Blood . . . My Love. ~~ Then My Joy will ripple through you, and you will know you are safe in My Arms. . . . Come, child, abide in Me, and I in you, and you will go out and bear much Fruit of My Spirit as you continue to be at rest . . . to listen . . . and abide."

June 23

If you love Me, you will obey what I command.
[JOHN 14:15]

May my tongue sing of Your Word, for all Your commands are righteous.
[PSALM 119:172]

"When I said, 'If you love Me, you will obey what I command,' I did not simply mean My 10 Commandments given to My people from Mount Sinai. No, it is much more than that. It is the little Whispers I speak to your heart. — Carrying out My Requests demonstrates your love for Me. Whatever you do, if you do it for My Glory, your love for Me shines through to Me, bringing Me great delight. A gentle nudge from Me, responded to with a singing heart, greatly warms My Heart."

June 24

A man of sorrows and acquainted with grief.
Surely He has borne our griefs and carried our sorrows.
[ISAIAH 53:3b,4a]

"Even in the sorrow and the pain ~~ especially in the sorrow and the pain ~~ I am with you, to comfort and defend you, to nurture and supply you with strength and courage. Remember, I am the Man of Sorrows and Pain ~~ acquainted with grief. ~~ I bore the weight of the sorrow and pain of mankind on My Shoulders ~~ and on My Heart. Only those who have borne deep sorrow and pain can have deep compassion for other sorrowing hearts. Run to My Arms of Love, and be held. The tears shed are a healing balm. . . . Let them flow from the depths of your heart. Only then can the healing begin. My Tears mingle with yours, completing that Healing Balm. . . . Rest in My Arms of Love . . . until My Peace puts your heart at rest. . . . Let the healing begin."

June 25

May the God of Peace, equip you with everything good for doing His Will, and may He work in us what is pleasing to Him, through Jesus Christ, to Whom be glory for ever and ever. Amen.
[HEBREWS 13:20-21]

May He turn our hearts to Him, to walk in all His Ways. And may these words of mine, which I have prayed before the LORD, be near to the LORD our God, that He may uphold His people according to each day's need.
[1 KINGS 8:58a,59]

"I will never lead you on a path . . . I will never direct you to complete a work — and then abandon you. Take courage, child. Whatever I lead you to do, I will empower You to do — I will equip you to do. You are My agent of change . . . My agent of Mercy . . . My agent of Love . . . My agent — equipped and empowered at every turn. Never fear. I am with you. I will uphold you according to each day's needs."

June 26

Let us draw near to God with a sincere heart.
[HEBREWS 10:22a]

My heart says of You, "Seek His Face!" Your Face, LORD, I will seek.
[PSALM 27:8]

"Spend time alone with Me, in My Inner Chambers, and you will learn more of Me — and be changed more completely — than during hours spent at the feet of scholars. Quality time spent with Me, seeking My Face — My Heart — My Words — My Touch, will change you — transform you — into a useful instrument of great worth in My Kingdom. Come now, and commune with Me, in My Inner Chambers. . . . You will be changed."

June 27

*I am going to send you what
My Father has promised.*
[LUKE 24:49a]

I will pour out My Spirit on all people.
[JOEL 2:28a]

*You will receive Power when the
Holy Spirit comes on you.*
[ACTS 1:8a]

"The 'religious' miss out on Intimacy with Me — and My Love Embrace. They seek to do a certain set of rules, or to flow on the wave of apathy and status quo. But My followers who truly seek Me, desire Me for Me — for all I Am — for all I have promised. Intimacy with Me must be your deepest desire. Expect Great Things from Me. Attempt Great Things for Me, through the Workings of My Spirit. Nothing done in your own power can have the Kingdom Impact of acts done through the Power of My Spirit, Living and Active in you. Seek Me — desire Me for the Impartation of My Spirit, and all that My Spirit has for you. When I left this earth, I proclaimed that you would receive My Power when My Spirit comes on you. . . . Be open. . . . Be filled. . . . Be empowered. . . . Be led. . . . Be used."

June 28

Have sincere love for your brothers,
love one another deeply, from the heart.
[1 PETER 1:22]

"My dear child, all sincere love comes from your Father. Align yourself closely with Me, and that Love, which I lavish on you, will flow through you onto those around you. They will see that you were made to pour out My Love onto them. And it will turn their hearts to Me. They will be overwhelmed with your sincere love, which flows deeply from your heart, when you have been with Me . . . embraced by My Love. It cannot fail to flow through you when you have been lavished with My Love, and you wait here in My Embrace, allowing your heart to be an open channel of My Love. Have sincere love for those I love. There is no greater calling."

June 29

I will rejoice in the LORD, I will be joyful in God my Savior.
The Sovereign LORD is my Strength.
[HABAKKUK 3:18,19a]

For the LORD your God is the One Who goes with you to fight for you against your enemies to give you victory.
[DEUTERONOMY 20:4]

Thanks be to God! He gives us the victory through our LORD Jesus Christ.
Therefore, my dear brothers, stand firm. Let nothing move you.
Always give yourselves fully to the work of the LORD.
[1 CORINTHIANS 15:57,58]

"Give Me all of yourself. Keep nothing back. Give Me your fears. . . . Give Me your pain. . . . Give Me all of you. Then I will give you My Authority to have dominion over the enemy, and to release the Manifest Presence of My Spirit. Not by your own words or your own power, but by My Power — My Spirit — that dwells in you. Fight FROM My Victory. Release My Power over _____. — Name that illness — that fear — that evil spirit — that rebellion — that relationship — that _____. Release the Power of My Victory over it. Now declare My Victory. Thank Me for that Victory. Thank Me for that healing. Thank Me for changing that evil to good. Thank Me for releasing you from that evil. Thank Me for the Victory. Praise Me for the Victory. Declare again that Victory. Claim that Victory. Speak it over and over. Speak the Victory in FULL MEASURE — not just what you think you are worthy of. Speak My Victory in FULL MEASURE. CLAIM IT! SPEAK IT! — DELCARE IT, OVER AND OVER! Give Me all of you. Watch My Manifest Power at work in your midst."

June 30

*Praise be to the Name of God for ever and
ever;
Wisdom and Power are His.
He reveals deep and hidden things.*
[DANIEL 2:20,22a]

"Seek Me. Seek to know Me, more and more. Seek to
know My Heart, My Wisdom, My Thoughts. I will reveal
deep and hidden things to those who seek Me with all
their heart — holding nothing back from Me. Come into
My Presence. I will speak My Truth to your listening ear.
I will reveal My Thoughts, My Character, My Nature, My
Love. Give Me your whole heart. And I will give you the
knowledge of the Wonders of My Kingdom. Come . . .
experience My Love, My Power, My Tender Touch . . .
each time revealing more of Me to your seeking heart. It
is My Deep Desire for My children to truly know Me . . .
deeply know Me, more and more."

July 1

You will fill me with Joy in Your Presence,
with eternal pleasures at Your Right Hand.
[PSALM 16:11b]

Come near to God and He will come near to
you.
[JAMES 4:8a]

He tends His flock like a shepherd:
He gathers the lambs in His Arms
and carries them close to His Heart.
[ISAIAH 40:11]

"Come into My Presence with thanksgiving in your heart. Come into My Presence, with that pain in your heart. Come into My Presence with joy in your heart. Come into My Presence, with that sorrow in your heart. Come into My Presence with laughter in your heart. Come into My Presence, with the mourning in your heart. Come into My Presence with deep worship flowing from your heart. Come into My Presence. Just come. And keep coming. More and more — come into My Presence. Just come. . . . My Loving Arms await you. . . . My Tender Touch awaits you. . . . My Welcoming Spirit awaits you. . . . My Healing Touch awaits you. . . . My Comfort awaits you. . . . My Peace awaits you. . . . My Joy awaits you. . . . My Warm Embrace awaits you. . . . My Healing awaits you. . . . My Love awaits you. . . . Just come. . . . My Forgiving Heart awaits you. . . . My Grace awaits you. . . . My Mercy awaits you. . . . My Loving Arms await you. . . . Just come. . . . My Presence awaits you."

July 2

Wait for the LORD;
be strong and take heart
and wait for the LORD.
[PSALM 27:14]

We wait in hope for the LORD;
He is our help and our shield.
In Him our hearts rejoice,
for we trust in His Holy Name.
May Your Unfailing Love rest upon us, O
LORD,
even as we put our hope in You.
[PSALM 33:20-22]

"Wait. Wait in hope for Me. Wait with strong trust in Me. Recall all the Wonders I have done for you, and for My people throughout the ages. Ponder over those miracles — those Wonders. And wait in hope for your miracle. Say, 'Father, I need a miracle.' And wait in hope, trusting Me to perform that miracle — in My Timing, My Design. Expect Great Things. Claim Great Things. Trust Me to act according to My Design for your life. . . . The waiting is part of the training. Learning to trust Me fully is a mark of maturity. Wait in hope for Me."

July 3

The LORD gives strength to His people;
the LORD blesses His people with peace.
[PSALM 29:11]

He gives strength to the weary, and increases
the power of the weak.
[ISAIAH 40:29]

O LORD my God, I called to You for help and
you healed me.
[PSALM 30:2]

"Strength, Power, Peace, health — My most sought-after Gifts. — Yours for the asking. The powers of darkness in this world seek to snuff out My people's strength, power, peace, and health. But I have overcome that darkness. Seek My Strength, My Power, My Peace, My Healing Touch. But more importantly, seek Me. In the darkest moments — in your weakest state — seek Me. And in so doing, My Gifts of Peace, Power, Strength, health are poured out in the measure of your need. And as you seek Me, My most treasured Gifts will also be poured into your heart. — Those most treasured Gifts are the Gift of My Presence, the Gift of My Love."

July 4

I will live in perfect freedom,
because I try to obey Your Teachings.
[PSALM 119:45 (GNT)]

Live as free men, but do not use your
freedom as a cover-up for evil; live as
servants of God.
[1 PETER 2:16]

You, my brothers, were called to be free.
But do not use your freedom to indulge the
sinful nature;
rather, serve one another in love.
[GALATIANS 5:13]

"Man's idea of freedom is so foreign to Mine. I came to set you free, so that you can walk in freedom from the oppression of evil, and have the freedom of walking with Me — not so that you can walk in the freedom of self-indulgence and every earthly evil desire — not so that you can demand your rights to do as you please, but so that you can do what pleases Me."

July 5

Do not let any unwholesome talk come out
of your mouths,
but only what is helpful for building others
up according to their needs.
Be kind and compassionate to one another,
forgiving each other, just as in Christ
God forgave you.
[EPHESIANS 4:29,32]

"When I was on earth, many marveled that no cruel talk came out of My Mouth — not even as I was being persecuted, flogged, and wrongfully accused — nor to the woman at the well. Do likewise, reflecting My Glory as you imitate Me and live as I lived, speak as I spoke, love as I loved, forgive as I forgave. There is no greater witness than for your life — your words — to reflect My Love."

July 6

*O LORD, You have searched me
and you know me.
You are familiar with all my ways.*
[PSALM 139:1,3b]

*You have said, 'I know you by name and you
have found favor with Me.'
If you are pleased with me, teach me Your
Ways so I may know You and continue to
find favor with You.*
[EXODUS 33:12b-13a]

*Know therefore that the LORD your God is
God;
He is the Faithful God, keeping His Covenant
of
Love to a thousand generations of those who
keep
His Commands.*
[DEUTERONOMY 7:9]

"Child, I have searched you and know you. Have you done the same with Me?? Have you searched Me with all your heart, so you may know My Ways, as I know yours? Know that I am the God Who keeps My Word to a thousand generations of those who follow after Me. I am He Whose Love is Unending. — Know what that truly means to you. Seek Me more and more, to deeply know Me more and more. I will reveal Myself to you as you watch Me at work in your midst. You will know My Heart when you see My Heart in action. You will know My Love when you see My Love in action. Be faithful to watch. Be faithful to follow Me, and to see Me in action. Avail yourself to Me. Avail yourself to the venues where I am allowed to show Myself Strong. Be open. Be willing. Be watchful. Know Me more and more."

July 7

*Since the creation of the world
God's invisible qualities
— His Eternal Power and Divine Nature —
have been clearly seen, being understood
from what has been made.*
[ROMANS 1:20]

"Look around. See My Majesty in the sunset. See Me in the beauty of the rose. See My Divine Nature in perfect DNA, in each smile, each color of the rainbow, each creature so unique. See My Power in the ocean. And know that I am He Who set it all in motion."

July 8

The Son is the radiance of God's Glory and the exact representation of His Being.
[HEBREWS 1:3]

He is the Image of the Invisible God. For God was pleased to have all His Fullness dwell in Him.
[COLOSSIANS 1:15a,19]

If you really knew Me, you would know My Father as well. From now on, you do know Him and have seen Him.
[JOHN 14:7]

"Father, Son, Spirit — the Three-In-One Trinity. What you see the Son having done here on earth in Scripture is the exact representation of the Godhead. The Father and Son are One. And now the Spirit is the exact representation of the Godhead, speaking the Truth to each heart, and accomplishing the Mighty Miracles the Son did on earth. One God, represented to mankind in three Forms. Know each Form, and you know the full extent of My Power, My WORD, My Majesty, My Glory, My Tenderness, My Love, My Compassion, My Touch."

July 9

[Yearning for God in the Midst of Distresses]
As the deer pants for the water brooks,
so pants my soul for You, O God.
[PSALM 42:1 (NKJV)]

I call on the LORD in my distress, and He
answers me.
[PSALM 120:1]

The LORD is near to all who call on Him.
[PSALM 145:18]

"When all looks lost look up. — Look up to Me. — Look up to My Welcoming Arms. Call out to Me. I am longing to hear your call. The call of one in need is a call for My Loving Hand. The nearer you walk with Me, the closer I am when you call. I know your need before you call, but the cry of your heart is a cry of trust — a cry of love for your Abba Father or your Dearest Friend. Look at it not as weakness when you call out to Me. I see it as the call of a heart yearning after Me — a heart yearning after the Tender Touch of your Father's Hand — a heart yearning for the Wisdom of your Master . . . the Gentle Embrace of your Loving Friend . . . the Comfort of My Listening Ear — a heart yearning after Me."

July 10

*I will listen to what God the LORD will say;
He promises Peace to His people.*
[PSALM 85:8a]

*In all your ways acknowledge Him, and He
will direct your paths.*
[PROVERBS 3:6]

Take time to think carefully about Jesus.
[HEBREWS 3:1b (WE)]

"I will not force My way into your life — into your schedule. I stand at the door of your heart, and knock for entrance. I entreat you to follow after Me — to let Me lead you on the path I've chosen for you — daily — moment by moment. Seek My Face and pursue Me. I am right here, waiting at the door of your heart. In your haste, do not ignore Me. In your vision for each day, do not ignore Me. I have much for you to do. I have much to say to you. I have much for you. . . . Do not ignore Me. Do not ignore My Kingdom Feast. Do not ignore My Heart of Love. Do not ignore My Whispers. . . . Do not ignore Me. I have much for you. . . . Do not ignore Me."

July 11

Honor your father and mother. Then you will live a long full life.
[EXODUS 20:12 (NLT)]

"Have you sought to honor your parents your whole life? That greatly pleases Me. That commandment is the only one with a promise. And I want to fulfill that promise for you. If your parents are two of My very dear people, and they have sought to follow Me all their lives, no greater legacy can be left. Leave that kind of legacy also — living a very full life in My service."

July 12

*Therefore, holy brothers, who share in the
heavenly calling,
fix your thoughts on Jesus.*
[HEBREWS 3:1]

*When He, the Spirit of Truth, comes, He will
guide you into all Truth.*
[JOHN 16:13]

"Give Me your moments. . . . It is only then that I will use you to the fullest. Focus your thoughts on Me. — Right now, focus your thoughts on Me. . . . Give Me a listening ear. . . . And keep a listening ear — listening for My Still Small Voice — My Whispers. . . . Even in the rush of the day, keep a listening ear for My Whispers. I will lead and direct your path. I will keep you focused on following My Will for your day. Be open to My Lead. Be open to My Whispers. . . . Fix your thoughts on Me."

July 13

After He had dismissed them, He went up on a mountainside by Himself to pray.
[MATTHEW 14:23a]

After leaving them, He went up on the mountainside to pray.
[MARK 6:46]

One of those days Jesus went out on the mountainside to pray, and spent the night praying to God.
[LUKE 6:12]

"Whenever you come to Me ~~ morning, noon or night ~~ I am here to meet with you. Do not be discouraged when other things distract you from spending time with Me. I have put many of those distractions ~~ those people ~~ in your path. Be not dismayed that your time was filled with them. I had My Purpose. That Purpose may not be clear to you now, but trust Me to bring it to pass. Yes, I want to have you here in My Presence, set apart for Me. But recall how I was pulled this way and that to touch the ill, the hurting, the lonely, the hungry, the lost. I withdrew to the mountainside alone, to pray to My Father. People kept pressing in for My Touch. But I made it a practice to run to the mountainside, even in the wee hours of the morning. That time alone with My Father was precious to Me in that human form. I know and understand how your heart yearns for more time in that Secret Place. As the day passes, and you still have not stolen away to that Secret Place, just call out to Me and I will comfort you and embrace you with My Love. I am here for you. Run to Me ~~ and My Embrace."

July 14

We have not stopped praying for you and asking God to fill you with the knowledge of His Will through all spiritual wisdom and understanding.
And we pray this in order that you may live a life worthy of the LORD and may please Him in every way: bearing fruit in every good work, growing in the knowledge of God.
[COLOSSIANS 1:9,10]

Let us know, let us pursue the knowledge of the LORD.
[HOSEA 6:3 (NASB)]

"Child, approach Me and ask Me to fill you with all wisdom and understanding, that you may know Me — deeply know Me — not just know about Me. I await your approach. It takes a depth of maturity to even know to ask. Knowing about Me is easy in your culture. Even the unbeliever can sometimes answer the question, 'Who is Jesus?' But only My pursuers can begin to know the depths of Who I am. Pursue Me and grow in your knowledge of Me. Pursue Me and know the depths of My Love for you. Pursue Me and know the depths of My Power available to you. Pursue Me and know Me more and more. Pursue Me."

July 15

*God once said, "Let light shine
out of the darkness!"
And this is the same God who made His light
shine in our hearts to let us know that His
own divine greatness is seen in the Face of
Christ.*

[2 CORINTHIANS 4:6 (ERV)]

"Come closer to the Light of My Glory. Let My Light shine into your heart so that I can reveal to you the Greatness of My Glory — the Greatness of My Divine Nature — the Greatness of My Love for you. Look into My Face and see the Light of My Glory shining forth. Look into My Face and see the Light of My Presence as you approach Me with praise. Look into My Face and see the Light of My Glory — the Light of My Power — that Power which is available at the sound of your praise. Praise Me and see the Light of My Glory — the Light of My Goodness — the Light of My Love warming your heart as you praise Me. Look into My Face. You will be changed."

July 16

But blessed are your eyes because they see,
and your ears because they hear.
For I tell you the truth, many prophets and
righteous men longed to see what you see
but did not see it, and to hear what you
hear but did not hear it.
[MATTHEW 13:16]

"Think how blessed you are to see the fulfillment of those prophecies of centuries ago. How blessed you are to read the very Words I spoke to the lost and hurting souls, and to My disciples. I still speak to My disciples who follow close to Me, yearning to hear My Words. I still appear to My disciples who look up at My Face as worship flows from hearts filled with love for Me. I still appear to you in the Mighty Power of the Touch of My Spirit when you seek My Touch as you lay hands on and pray for the sick. Think how blessed you are. Give thanks to Me from a grateful heart for choosing you to be one of My disciples. Come. Follow Me. Hear the Words of Life flowing from My Lips. See the Power of My Touch."

July 17

Let us rejoice and be glad and give Him glory!
For the wedding of the Lamb has come, and His Bride has made herself ready.
[REVELATION 19:7]

Live in harmony with one another.
If it is possible, as far as it depends on you, live at peace with everyone.
[ROMANS 12:16a,18]

Live a life of love.
[EPHESIANS 5:2a]

"My great desire is for My people — My Body — My Bride — to dwell together in harmony with one another. Live a life of love. Be filled with My Love, and be a source of My Love, My Life, My Peace, My Joy . . . My Love. Bear much fruit — for the joining together of My people in love and peace. Bear much fruit — for the edification of My people, and for the lost ones I place in your path. My Bride must make herself ready."

July 18

But it was because the LORD loved you. . .
[DEUTERONOMY 7:8a]

. . .because the LORD your God loves you.
[DEUTERONOMY 23:5]

Because of the LORD's eternal love. . .
[1 KINGS 10:9]

Because the LORD loves His people. . .
[2 CHRONICLES 2:11]

Because of the LORD's great love we are not consumed,
for His compassions never fail.
[LAMENTATIONS 3:22]

And hope does not disappoint us, because God has poured out His Love into our hearts by the Holy Spirit, Whom He has given us.
[ROMANS 5:5]

Because of His Great Love for us, God, Who is rich in mercy, made us alive in Christ.
[EPHESIANS 2:4,5a]

Love must be sincere. Be devoted to one another in brotherly love. Honor one another above yourselves. Live in harmony with one another.
[ROMANS 12:9,10,12,16a]

"Love. . . . Love. . . . That is the basis of both My Old and New Covenants with My people. I am Love. Love defines Me. Love defines — Love explains — all that I am, all that I do and have done for My people. Then you say, 'But if You are a Loving God, why did that person have to die — why did that tragic thing happen??' My Love is Pure. My Love is Righteous. My Love is Unconditional. But My Love is also Just. Out of My Love, I discipline My children as a loving father disciplines his children, to train them up in the way they should go. And I gave the gift of freedom of choice to all mankind. The enemy lurks to seek and devour all who have not chosen Me — and also all of My children, since he desires death and destruction of all who follow Me. This is a fallen world. Therefore, evil abounds. When Adam and Eve chose to eat the fruit from the Tree of the Knowledge of Good and Evil, it became clear that I am a God of Justice and will therefore deliver what My warning had declared — that man must surely die. But when you choose to follow Me, My Love is freely poured out on you to comfort and embrace you throughout this life's sometimes difficult journey. My Love is the key. Rely on My Love to make good out of evil — to empower My people to live in peace and harmony with one another — loving one another deeply from the heart. Love . . . My Love . . . That is the defining theme of My Covenant with you. May it also be the defining theme of your covenant with Me and with My people. Love . . . My Love . . . My Love explains it all."

July 19

May the God of Peace. . .equip you with
everything good for doing His Will.
[HEBREWS 13:20-21]

"You are precious. I created you to be My disciple —
equipped with My special gifting to reach this world for
Me. Go forward, unafraid. I am with you. I am Mighty
to save — to save, not only from eternal damnation —
to save you now, from the darkness that looms around
you — and around those lost souls I put in your path.
Go forward, unafraid. I will go with you. I will provide
for you the tools of My Kingdom. Use them. I will show
you how. — Step by step, I will lead you. Rest secure in
My Love, My Grace, My Power — Ever-present — always
near. Go forward, unafraid. Rest secure in My Peace that
surpasses your knowledge right now. It will be revealed
to you in abundance, as you walk with Me and rest secure
in My Arms. I love you. . . . My Peace I give to you. Run
in My Strength. Sense My Presence here with you. Rest
secure in My Love."

July 20

Bear with each other and forgive whatever grievances you have against one another. Forgive as the LORD forgave you.
[COLOSSIANS 3:13]

"Forgiveness — no greater gift to mankind — no greater gift you can give to one another. True forgiveness holds no grudge. True forgiveness desires no retribution — no retaliation. True forgiveness lets go of the offense. True forgiveness does not necessarily pronounce the offense non-offensive, but you must let go of the offense. No, the pain may not be erased, but you must let go of allowing that offense to continue to torture you. Each time Satan reminds you of it, once again tell Me you forgive that offender, and turn that offender over to Me for My Judgment. You must let it go. Let Me be the Judge. Once that is complete, the one set free is really you. You are set free from letting that offense — and that offender — have control over you. Give it all to Me. Be set free. I love you, child. I set you free."

July 21

Serve wholeheartedly, as if you were serving the LORD, not men.
[EPHESIANS 6:7]

This service that you perform is not only supplying the needs of God's people but is also overflowing in many expressions of thanks to God.
[2 CORINTHIANS 9:12]

"Serve others. That was My example to My first disciples. Service accomplishes much — so much more than the task at hand. Service done as unto Me tenderizes the heart of the servant. Service done out of a prideful heart, though, serves only to puff up the servant, and can actually cause a breakdown of My Kingdom. Only service done as unto Me, out of a heart consecrated to Me, furthers My Kingdom, and shines My Light into the darkness. Service done out of a grateful heart displays My Kingdom to the world. So go child. Serve as unto Me, and be a beacon of My Light and the touch of My Love on the lives and hearts around you. Joy will be your great reward."

July 22

Rend your clothes, and gird you with sackcloth, and mourn before Abner.
[2 SAMUEL 3:31 (KJV)]

"Even now," declares the LORD, "return to Me with all your heart, with fasting and weeping and mourning."
Rend your heart and not your garments.
Return to the LORD your God, for He is gracious and compassionate, slow to anger and
abounding in love.
[JOEL 2:12-13]

"Child, when your heart is breaking, seek My Face. Seek My Arms of Love — My Heart of Mercy and Grace. Then humbly open your heart to Me. You must search your heart for any darkness — any pride — any self — any fear — any doubt — anything that separates you from Me. Write down those areas of darkness, as you confess from your repentant heart. Now rend that paper into shreds, as in days long ago when My people would rend their garment as an act of repentance and sorrow. You are now set free from that darkness that covered and filled your heart. Come back into My Arms and let Me finish the healing of your repentant, broken heart. . . . Bask in My Love and Compassion. My Love makes all things new."

July 23

*Choose for yourselves this day whom you shall serve. . . .
As for me and my household, we will serve the LORD.*
[JOSHUA 24:15b]

*You cannot serve two masters at the same time. You will hate one and love the other, or you will be loyal to one and not care about the other.
You cannot serve God and Money at the same time.*
[MATTHEW 6:24 (ERV)]

*Their god is their stomach. . . .
Their mind is on earthly things.*
[PHILIPPIANS 3:19]

Blessed are those who hunger and thirst after righteousness, for they will be filled.
[MATTHEW 5:6]

"Choose this day whom you shall serve. . . . God, or mammon, or **self**. . . . Is your god the 'almighty' dollar and all that money buys? . . . Is your god your stomach? . . . Is your god that addiction? . . . Is your god other people? Or **self**? . . . Is your god TV, movies, Facebook, or other media?? . . . Whatever captures you heart and dominates your attention — whatever you place first— whatever devours your time and governs you — that is your god of those moments. I want to be not just a god among other gods in your life. I want to be the God of gods — LORD of lords — King of kings — Almighty Master — your One True God! When you choose other gods you lose so much of yourself — your potential — your dignity — your Anointing — your Blessings — your Provision. And you lose so much of Me — your Guardian — your Shepherd — your Lover — your Friend. . . . Choose this day whom you shall serve."

July 24

This doesn't mean, of course, that we have only a hope of future joys — we can be full of joy here and now even in our trials and troubles. Taken in the right spirit these very things will give us patient endurance; this in turn will develop a mature character, and a character of this sort produces a steady hope, a hope that will never disappoint us. Already we have some experience of the love of God flooding through our hearts by the Holy Spirit given to us.

[ROMANS 5:3-5 (PHILLIPS)]

The crowd joined in the attack against Paul and Silas, and the magistrates ordered them to be stripped and beaten. After they had been severely flogged, they were thrown into prison. About midnight Paul and Silas were praying and singing hymns to God.

[ACTS 16:22,23b,25]

"Look to Me when troubles assail you. I am the Author and Finisher of your faith. Trust Me to lead you and guide you, and to keep you in My Care. Along this tiresome road, are many opportunities for you to grow — to mature — to deepen your faith, and to trust more in Me. Look at Paul as your example. His trials and sufferings made him into a mighty man of God. He suffered torment and imprisonment— but through it all, was able to see the reward for his faith as he praised Me from His prison cell, and souls were won for Me. In your daily battles — even in your roughest storms — if you can turn to Me with trust in your heart, and let Me banish your fears and build your faith, you will reap great rewards. Those rewards may not seem evident right now, but praise Me in advance and you will look back and see the vast strides — the many blessings — the great rewards for your present sufferings. Trust Me to make all things new."

July 25

Show me Your Ways, O LORD, teach me Your Paths;
guide me in Your Truth and teach me, for You are my Savior, and my hope is in You all day long.
According to Your Love remember me, for You are Good, O LORD.
[PSALM 25:4,5,7b]

We wait in hope for the LORD; He is our help and our Shield.
May Your unfailing Love rest upon us, O LORD,
even as we put our hope in You.
[PSALM 33:20,22]

Why are you so downcast, O my soul?
Put your hope in God.
[PSALM 42:5,11; 43:5]

"Hope. . . .Hope is your sole source of strength when all seems lost. When hope is lost, all is lost. But put your hope in Me, and I will see you through the trials and pain and suffering. Put your hope in Me, and I will fill you with strength, and supply you with wisdom, favor and honor. Put your hope in Me, and I will increase your endurance and faith. Put your hope in Me, and I will give you patience to endure the wait. Put your hope in Me. There is no sweeter promise for peace and My Love."

July 26

Therefore I tell you, do not worry about your life.
[MATTHEW 6:25a]

Do not worry beforehand about what to say. Just say whatever is given to you at the time, for it is not you speaking, but the Holy Spirit.
[MARK 13:11b]

The LORD is my strength and my Shield; my heart trusts in Him and I am helped.
[PSALM 28:7a]

I sought the LORD, and He answered me; He delivered me from all my fears.
[PSALM 34:4]

"Fear, worry, fret — — all are a signal of lack of trust in Me. I hear you saying, 'LORD, I trust You fully. — It's me I don't trust. I'm too weak, too inadequate for the job, too. . .' But, child, can you trust Me to give you the needed strength? — the needed wisdom? — the needed favor? Can you trust Me? If so, there are no limits to all I can do through you. Just trust Me. Give Me your worries, your fears, your anxious thoughts. Trust Me to bring redemption to it all."

July 27

Look to the LORD and His Strength;
seek His Face always.
[1 CHRONICLES 16:11 / PSALM 105:4]

When Your WORDS came, I ate them;
They were my joy and my heart's delight.
[JEREMIAH 15:16]

The Spirit gives Life.
The WORDS I have spoken to you are Spirit
and
they are Life.
[JOHN 6:63]

"Be swift to hear Me, even as I am swift to hear your pleas. Run after My Precepts. . . . Seek My Face. . . . Seek My WORDS of Life. . . . Seek My WORDS of Love. . . . Seek My WORDS of Wisdom, Strength, and Security. I was the WORD made flesh. . . . Seek Me. Be swift to hear My WORDS now whispered into your listening ear. And be swift to answer with your love and praise."

July 28

He took the children in His Arms.
[MARK 10:16a]

*See, the Sovereign LORD comes with Power.
He tends His flock like a shepherd:
He gathers the lambs in His Arms and
carries them close to His Heart.*
[ISAIAH 40:10a,11]

*As for you, the anointing you received from
Him remains in you.*
[1 JOHN 2:27a]

"You are My child, My servant, My friend — whom I seek to companion with. I want to hold you tightly. — Do not resist the Arms that seek to carry you. That is My desire, child — to hold you tightly and carry you close to My Heart. I hold out My Hand as a Friend. . . . Come into My Arms. . . . Love and be Loved. . . . Be lovingly held. . . . Be listened to, and encouraged. . . . Be nurtured. . . . Be held. And I hold out My Scepter as a King. . . . Come into My Throne Room. . . . Be strengthened. . . . Be anointed for service. . . . Be touched by My Power. . . . Be empowered to serve Me. . . . And be led."

July 29

*"My Presence will go with you,
and I will give you rest."*
[EXODUS 33:14]

*Find rest, O my soul, in God alone;
my hope comes from Him.*
[PSALM 62:5]

"Come, child. Be still. Rest in My Arms. Come — closer and closer to Me, and I will give you that rest for your soul that you so desire. Rest, child, rest. Give yourself totally to Me. Sit with Me at the start of every day. Then, and only then, will your day, your activities, your efforts flow smoothly — done in a restful, peaceful manner. Sit with Me, child, and then go forth, flying on wings like eagles — lifting you higher and higher. Go in My Peace . . . in My Strength."

July 30

And the LORD has declared this day that you are
His treasured possession.
[DEUTERONOMY 26:18]

"Child, you are My treasured possession. I want you closer and closer to Me. Every day I want to hold you close — so close that you feel the Heartbeat of My Spirit flowing into your innermost being. Fix your eyes, your thoughts, your heart on Me. I want our eyes to meet more often. . . . Ponder these thoughts. . . . Just wait before Me. When you are at rest, you can more easily hear My Words to you. Be still. Just be Mine. Child, you are Mine. That is what gives you worth. You are Mine, child. You are Mine to hold — to hold very still — until all your fears are washed away. You are Mine — You are My treasured possession."

July 31

I tell you the Truth, whatever you bind on earth will be bound in heaven, and whatever you loose on earth will be loosed in heaven.
[MATTHEW 18:18]

"I am yours — you are Mine. Together we form a team to loose the chains around you and those dear ones you lift up to Me in prayer. You are My friend — I am yours. I know the plans I have for you — plans to give you a rich future full of Life — My Life, My Spirit, My Presence. Run away with Me from the cares of this world. You are Mine. I set you free when you take My Hand and follow Me."

Aug. 1

*I love You, O L*ORD*, my Strength.*
[PSALM 18:1]

"Life with Me — intimacy with Me — truly is a Love Story. Come. Sit with Me. Experience My Love flowing from My Heart into yours — healing — mending your broken heart. Lay all your burdens on Me. Be set free from all the weight of this world. I paid the ultimate price to set you free from those chains that bind you to this world. Bow down to Me and be set free from strife, loneliness, brokenness. Come to Me, child, and be set free — set free to love and be loved."

Aug. 2

Be imitators of God, therefore, as dearly loved children, and live a life of love, just as Christ loved us and gave Himself up for us as a fragrant offering and sacrifice to God.
[EPHESIANS 5:1-2]

"Yes, child, your *OWN* love is faulty, but when your channel is unblocked, you are My conduit of Love that heals the broken-hearted, the desperate, the depressed, the lonely, the fearful. You are My instrument →My Hands, My Feet, My Listening Ear to carry My Love to the hearts and lives of the hurting, the fearful, the unloved. Reach out and touch them with My Love. Go forward, unafraid. — My Perfect Love casts away all your fears, when you do not allow the enemy a foothold. Rest in My Peace. . . .Then go forth in My Love."

Aug. 3

How precious to me are Your Thoughts, O God!
[PSALM 139:17a]

"When your heart's desire is to be with Me, to hear from Me, to learn from Me . . . to just be near Me . . . you can then walk with Me — close to Me — along life's journeys, which I have prepared in advance for you. Open My WORD and let Me enlighten those WORDS meant just for you. Fall more in love with My WORD. You will never be the same. It will change you. It will change your focus on life . . . change your heart . . . change the meditations of your heart. Come to My Banqueting Table. Feast on My Meat. You will never be the same."

Aug. 4

These words are the secret to life and health to all who discover them.
[PROVERBS 4:22 (ERV)]

"Come to Me, all you who are weary and burdened, and I will give you rest."
[MATTHEW 11:28]

My soul finds rest in God alone; my salvation comes from Him.
Find rest, O my soul, in God alone; my hope comes from Him.
[PSALM 62:1,5]

O God, You are my God, earnestly I seek You; my soul thirsts for you.
I have seen you in the sanctuary and beheld Your Power and Your Glory.
Because Your Love is better than life, my lips will glorify You.
Because of Your help, I sing in the shadow of Your Wings.
My soul clings to You; Your Right Hand upholds me.
With singing lips my mouth will praise you.
[PSALM 63:1a,3,4,7,8,5b]

"My beloved child, rest in the Secret Place of the Almighty. Here you find rest for your soul when you abide here. No rushing in, to just lay out your requests. Abide in this Secret Place with Me. No, you need not be physically at rest — but your spirit, your inner self, must be at rest. For what is the cause of unrest? — self. Self must be put at rest here in My Presence. Come unto Me, and I will give you that Rest — Rest for your spirit, for your soul, for your heart. Fix your thoughts on Me. Then you will hear My Voice calling in the wilderness, 'Come unto Me, and I will give you Rest.' Rest and Peace, and also Joy will permeate your very being. . . . Peace . . . turning into unspeakable Joy . . . deep within your soul. Shower that Joy, that Peace, that Love, onto all you encounter, as you go forth from this Secret Place."

Aug. 5

*Look to the LORD and His Strength;
seek His Face always.*
[PSALM 105:4]

*Trust in the LORD with all your heart and
lean not on your own understanding.*
[PROVERBS 3:5]

*The LORD takes delight in His faithful
followers,
and in those who wait for His loyal love.*
[PSALM 147:11 (NET)]

"Trials that you bring to Me to fix — out of your trust in Me — out of your love for Me — are what bring Me Joy from My friends. It is those trials you choose to deal with on your own — with no need of Me, no desire for Me, no regard for Me — that bring Me pain. The nails are driven deeper with each disobedience, each distrust, each time I am ignored by My friends. Turn to Me — even in the littlest trials of the day — and bring Joy to My Heart in that turning."

Aug. 6

Holy brothers, who share in the heavenly calling, fix your thoughts on Jesus.
[HEBREWS 3:1]

You have made known to me the paths of life;
you will fill me with joy in Your Presence.
[PSALM 16:11 / ACTS 2:28]

"Yes, child, fix your thoughts on Me — on My Purposes for you, My Plans for you — My Presence with you, My Love for you. Let Me quiet you with My Love. When you allow My Light, My Love, to warm you — to warm you here in My Presence — you will never be the same. I love you, child. Think on these things."

Aug. 7

We wait in hope for the LORD; He is our Help and our Shield.
[PSALM 33:20]

The LORD your God is with you,
He is Mighty to save. . . .
He will quiet you with His Love.
[ZEPHANIAH 3:17]

"Rest in My Arms and let Me quiet you with My Love. Each delay is a lesson in trust. Can you trust Me to provide for you? When all looks lost, can you trust Me? The wait makes the answers even more precious. Wait and see. I love you. I love to provide for your every need. Trust Me."

Aug. 8

My purpose is that they may be encouraged in heart and united in love, so that they may have the full riches of complete understanding, in order that they may know the mystery of God, namely, Christ, in Whom are hidden all the treasures of wisdom and knowledge.
[COLOSSIANS 2:2-3]

He graciously gave me the privilege of telling the Gentiles about the endless treasures available to them in Christ.
[EPHESIANS 3:8]

"I give you the treasures of My Kingdom. But not only that, I give you My Love, Myself, My Companionship. Take My Hand and let Me lead you into My Storehouse of Treasures — Treasures beyond your imagining. And most of all, take My Hand and let Me walk with you, and carry you when your strength fails you. For where you are weak, I am strong — when you allow My Strength to carry you. Seek Me first, and then all My Treasures are yours. I love you deeply. Come with Me — whole-heartedly come with Me. Let Me unlock the Storehouse of My Treasures for you. Claim big things from My Treasures. You are a child of the King. Come, collect your Inheritance now."

Aug. 9

*I will instruct you and teach you in the way
you should go;
I will counsel you and watch over you.*
[PSALM 32:8]

*My sheep listen to My Voice;
I know them, and they follow Me.*
[JOHN 10:27]

"To the open, humble, and contrite heart, I speak volumes. Keep the ears of your spirit attuned to My Voice. Yes, child, I will speak and you will hear when you are still. As you sit in silence, fixing the eyes of your heart on Me, listen, child, and you will hear WORDS of Life pulsing through your very being. Listen, child, listen and you will know what it really means to commune with Me, Your LORD and Savior — your Loving Shepherd. My sheep hear My Voice and follow My leading. I love you, little lamb."

Aug. 10

I can do everything through Him
Who gives me strength.
[PHILIPPIANS 4:13]

"Yes, child, you can do all things I direct you to do. Wait, though, until the given time to act. Be alert to My leading and do not run ahead of Me. Doing things on your own time frame — going ahead of Me, trying to work things out and make things happen in your own strength will result in huge blessings missed — both in your own life and in the lives of all who are touched by your actions. Submit to My Leadership and wait. . . .Wait for My Hand to act on your behalf. I love you, child. I will never forsake you."

Aug. 11

I will listen to what God the LORD will say; He promises peace to His people.
[PSALM 85:8a]

"Sitting at My Feet is not the only times I speak to your heart, deep spiritual truths. If your thoughts are racing or you are stressed about your work load, you will never hear Me then. But even as you do your daily tasks, talk to Me — friend to Friend. Then you can hear My Voice if you tune the ears of your spirit to My Still Small Voice. Then heed My WORDS, and all is well with your soul. Say it, 'It is well with my soul.' — Say it until your inner being echoes it back to you. 'All is well with my soul when My LORD — my Friend — my Savior speaks, and I listen, and I obey and walk His directed path for me.' Say it until your spirit is at rest. Then truly, all is well."

Aug. 12

The LORD has declared this day that you are His people, His treasured possession.
[DEUTERONOMY 26:18]

"You are Mine. . . .You are loved. . . .You are cared for. . . . You are nourished. . . . You are blessed. . . . You are cherished. . . . You are Mine — My treasured possession."

Aug. 13

Find rest, O my soul, in God alone; my hope comes from Him.
[PSALM 62:5]

"Reaching that calm, that rest, is not as difficult as you often make it. Stop and seek My Face and come into My Presence. . . . Be still — here in My Inner Chamber — and you will surely find that rest for your weary soul. Come. . . . Come. . . . Rest in My Arms of Love. . . . Now, go do My Will, in peace. You will be richly blessed."

Aug. 14

Teach me Your Way, O LORD, and I will walk in Your Truth; give me an undivided heart, that I may fear Your Name.
[PSALM 86:11]

"There is more for you to discover, more to be revealed to you, more for you to learn and act on. Do not sit idly by, and think I cannot act on your behalf, or that I have forgotten you. — Quite the opposite!!! I am acting on your behalf more than you can ever imagine! Keep close to Me. Watch and wait. You will see My Glory displayed in your life. Watch and wait, ever seeking My Face. Bow down in worship and praise, and watch My Hand act in your life — in your heart. Watch and wait."

Aug. 15

I have love you with an Everlasting Love;
I have drawn you with Loving-Kindness.
[JEREMIAH 31:3]

Mary sat at the LORD's feet,
listening to what He taught.
But Martha was distracted by the big dinner
she
was preparing.
[LUKE 10:39-40a]

"Sit at My Feet before you rise for the day. Be Mary, not Martha first. When you start your day with My Strength upholding you, your day will be much sweeter. — Even with many interruptions and time-killers, you will have the strength to carry on and be guided with joy and thanks and praise. Even a few moments alone with Me will set your spirit free. — You will know your strength is from My Power at work in your life — in your heart — in your spirit. Cling to Me and I will put your soul at rest and you will be empowered by My Spirit at work in your heart — at work in your life. Let Me use you to will and to work according to My Dear Purposes for you. Watch, child, you will see great Wonders unfold. Be still. Be at rest. Be Mine."

Aug. 16

May Your Unfailing Love rest upon me, O LORD, even as I put my hope in You.
[PSALM 33:22]

"The Power of My Love flows through you when you turn to Me and wait for My Presence to come fill you and surround you. Be still and know that I am here with you — in Tenderness, in Power. Loose that Power to cleanse you, to wash you clean so you are an open channel of My Love, My Healing Power, My Joy and Peace. . . . Wait now in My Presence for My Life to flow through you. . . . Be still . . . and wait."

Aug. 17

I have heard your prayers and seen your tears,
I will heal you.
[2 KINGS 20:5]

"I have seen your many tears, and I have heard the deep heart-cries from your broken, hurting heart. Child, I love you. I am here to heal your broken heart. Never fear. Never doubt that I am working all things for your ultimate good. Some of My most treasured blessings are those that take time to put into place. I see the completed tapestry. — You however, only see the tangled threads dangling from your heart. Trust Me to make your life into a beautiful tapestry. Others have seen the beauty appearing. Press on for the treasure ahead. Trust Me to lead you there, along a steady path. Treasures await."

Aug. 18

I trust in Your Unfailing Love, my heart rejoices in Your salvation.
[PSALM 13:5]

Be imitators of God, therefore, as dearly loved children and live a life of love.
[EPHESIANS 5:1,2a]

"Pour out My Love on each one I bring into your pathway. Just be a channel — unblocked by self, unblocked by pride, unblocked by fear. Washed clean with My Blood, you are My conduit of Love. Be available. Be used. And in turn, you are filled and surrounded with My Love, and the love of those you touch. Think of it. A life filled with Love. Life with Me truly is a Love story. Fall deeper in Love with Me."

Aug. 19

*Seek the LORD while He may be found; call
on Him while He is near.*
[ISAIAH 55:6]

"Take My Hand. Let Me lead you and guide you, and walk close beside you on the path I have planned and prepared for you. With a yielded heart, a yielded spirit ~~ as a small child looks up expectantly and reaches out their hand for yours ~~ take My Hand and follow Me. ~~ Feel My Love flowing through that grasp, knowing all is well, trusting Me at every turn. Joy and Peace will fill your yielded heart."

Aug. 20

Consider the Great Love of the LORD.
[PSALM 107:43b]

"Come, child, come sit at My Feet as I reveal My Secrets, My Truths, My Heart to you. Listen. . . . Listen for My Call. Come quickly to My Side, and there you will find all you need . . . Love, Strength, Power, Comfort, Healing, Peace, Protection. Then wait with Me, Your Friend, Your Dearest Companion. Wait with Me in the silence, yielded and still, as you behold My Glory. Wait for the full measure of My Love to fill you. Now go forth. And share My Love with all you meet."

Aug. 21

No longer do I call you slaves, for the slave does not know what his master is doing; but I have called you friends.
[JOHN 15:15 (NASB)]

"I am your Friend — your Dearest Companion. Come close to Me for all you need — Love, Understanding, a Listening Ear, Support, Provision, Strength, Protection, Joy — your All in All. Sit here first in silence. . . . Then with free abandon, tell Me your deepest secrets. Reveal what lies hidden in your heart. Then wait in silence for My Peace to set you free — free from guilt and shame — free from fears and failure — free from worry and stress — free from selfish thoughts, selfish demands. Be filled instead with trust and My Peace. So come to My Waiting Open Arms. . . . So come."

Aug. 22

*The LORD your God is with you, He is Mighty
to save. . . .
He will quiet you with His Love.*
[ZEPHANIAH 3:17]

"Lay your burdens, your fears, your doubts at My Feet.
There receive My Blessings of Peace, Strength, and
Power. It is in My Keeping-Power, that you shall find rest
for your soul — your very inner being. Let go of the past.
Past failures, confessed, are washed away as far as the east
is from the west. You must forgive yourself. And now, let it
go. Thank Me for My Forgiveness, rather than chastising
yourself for those past failures. Claim My Keeping-Power
to keep you from all evil and harm, to calm the storm
around you, to calm the storm within you. Rest in that
Peace."

Aug. 23

Give thanks to the LORD, call on His Name;
let the hearts of those who seek the LORD
rejoice.
[PSALM 105:1a,3b]

"Give thanks to Me first, praising Me for Who I Am, for what I have done for you in your past struggles. Then, child, lay your requests before Me. Then rejoice in knowing I will answer your call.

My Divine order→ Praise and thanksgiving open the door to My inner sanctuary; there you lay down your burdens and seek My Face and call on My Name; then go forth rejoicing as you trust Me fully to supply, to protect, to care, to meet your needs. Practice this until it becomes part of who you are in Me. . . . Praise – Ask – Rejoice. . . . Do it, child, and marvels will unfold. Praise – Ask – Rejoice. . . . Do it daily.

Praise – Ask – Rejoice. . . . Moment by moment . . . Do it until your first response to Me is praise, out of a thankful heart. Praise – Ask – Rejoice. . . . Do it until it defines who you are in Me. Praise – Ask – Rejoice . . . these three. And the greatest of these is Praise. Let praise be ever on your lips."

Aug. 24

We wait in hope for the LORD; He is our Help and
our Shield.
In Him our hearts rejoice,
for we trust in His Holy Name.
[PSALM 33:20-21]

"You are the object of My Love. Go forth in My Presence.
Go forth unafraid.
Know that I Am. . . .

    I Am your Lover.

    I Am your Guide.

    I Am your Redeemer, your King.

    I Am your Dearest Friend.

    I Am your Peace, your Provider, your Creator.

    I Am your Strength, your Joy, the Object of your
praise.

    I give you songs of deliverance in the night, in the
quietness.

    I Am He Who was promised.

. . . I Am. . . ."

Aug. 25

Look to the LORD and His Strength;
seek His Face always.
[1 CHRONICLES 16:11]

"As you walk with Me through life's various journeys, your need, your desire, your love for Me changes and transpires. Your love — kindled by your need of Me . . . . Your desire — kindled by your love for Me. . . . Your love — kindled by your desire for Me. . . .

Think back to what has brought you nearest to Me . . . joys, sorrows, fears, peace, loss, gain. . . . Each has had its reward as you came nearer and nearer to Me — your Life-Flow. That nearness, that intimacy we've shared, is My design for Kingdom Living. Moment by moment, draw nearer to Me. No matter the circumstances, set your heart on being near Me. Join Me now, dear child, in My Inner Chamber. And remember, you are a temple of My Holy Spirit. Within you is My Inner Chamber. Commune with Me now — spirit to Spirit."

Aug. 26

*How great is the Love the Father
has lavished on us.*
[1 JOHN 3:1a]

*((Abba Father, just to think of Your
Love being lavished on me sets my heart
soaring.))*

"Think only of Me when you face the struggles of this life. In thinking of Me, of My Love, of My Faithfulness, it will set your heart at rest. Then joy will flood your heart. Your very innermost being will be set free to love Me in return. Come, companion with Me in the midst of strife, fears, failures. Darkness will be revealed, and you will be set free when you repent of those dark ways. I wrap you, then, in My Love, and carry you close to My Heart. What sweet Peace will enter your soul and set your heart at rest. My Love sets you free. Stay close. Love Me with all your heart, soul, mind, spirit. My Love is freely given to you. Take My Hand and come closer and closer to Me, enwrapped in My Love. Come. Take My Hand. Come into My Inner Chamber. Love awaits you there."

Aug. 27

*I wait for You, O LORD; You will answer,
O LORD my God.*
[PSALM 38:15]

"I hear your every cry, I listen to every plea. Sometimes My answer is, 'Yes, so be it.' Sometimes it will be, 'No.' I know the hardest answer for you to sometimes hear, though, is, 'Wait, child.' Trust Me. Wait till all things work together for your good and for the good of those whose lives are also touched. Be ever sure of My Healing Touch, My Strength to act, My Desire to care for your every need. Ask and it shall be given unto you, good measure, pressed down. Seek My Face, seek My Hand, seek My Love. Trust in My Unfailing Love. Rest in My Love. . . . My Tender-Loving Care is yours for the asking. Seek it above all else. Turn to Me at every turn. Let Me hold you close. Know that I am here ~~ ever present, always near. Protected and cherished, do not fear. Know all is well."

Aug. 28

Yet this I call to mind and therefore I have hope:
Because of the LORD's great Love we are not consumed, for His Compassions never fail.
They are new every morning;
great is Your Faithfulness.
[LAMENTATIONS 3:21-23]

"Fresh and new every morning is My Love, is My Compassion . . . My Provision . . . My Forgiveness . . . My Presence . . . My WORD. Draw unto Me in fresh awareness of Me and all I am for you — all I am to you. Trust in My Unfailing Love. Therein will you live the promised Abundant Life — free of worry . . . free of guilt . . . free of sorrow . . . free of loneliness and fear — when you lay those burdens at My Feet. Come before Me with singing, and I will provide you songs of deliverance to fill your heart with joy and peace. Come before Me with joyful adoration, out of a heart fully-fixed on finding My Treasures. Dig deep into My WORD. Hide it in your heart, and then I will bring it to mind at the very moment you need it. Dig deep for those Priceless Treasures, given centuries ago, and yet alive and active today. Hide them in your heart. Priceless Treasures, new every morning."

Aug. 29

If you have any encouragement from being united with Christ, if any comfort from His Love, if any fellowship with the Spirit, if any tenderness and compassion, then make my joy complete by being like-minded, having the same Love.
[PHILIPPIANS 2:1,2]

"I love you, child. I see in your heart, tenderness for the hurting. I put that there, and I am training you to act out of mercy and love and compassion with My hurting lambs, and those you meet who I put in your path. A tender heart is My Heart's desire for each of My children. You were formed in the likeness of Me — Tender-hearted, Compassionate, Unconditionally Loving My people. Model that in your daily living. And you will be filled with deep joy, as you touch each one with My Love!!!"

Aug. 30

*Humble yourselves, therefore,
under God's Mighty Hand,
that He may lift you up in due time.*
[1 PETER 5:6]

"Humble yourself before Me, that I may lift you up in due time. You will be used mightily in My Kingdom when you humble yourself as a servant — seeking to do My Will only. When you worry about what others think of you, that is pride. Rid yourself quickly of pride and look only into My Eyes, and see total Acceptance and Love. Seek only after that — not the glory of man. Look only into My Eyes with a humble, contrite heart, and I will lift you up. **Self**-assurance — replaced by MY Assurance — keeps your heart humble. You know then from whence your worth comes, from Whom your Strength comes, from Whom your acceptance comes, from Whom your confidence comes, from Whom your life comes. Take pride only in Me — your Redeemer. Out of My Love and Mercy, I am your Redeemer — your Deliverer, your Avenger. I guarantee your freedom to act according to My Will for your life. And I secure your future, as you continue to humble yourself and pray, and seek My Face."

Aug. 31

I will rejoice in the LORD, I will be joyful in
God my Savior.
The Sovereign LORD is my Strength;
He makes my feet like the feet of a deer,
He enables me to go on the heights.
[HABAKKUK 3:18-19]

"When you can praise Me in times of pain and suffering, I immediately act to bring you relief — perhaps not in the way you expect, but relief nevertheless. When you can praise Me in the storm, and trust Me to deliver you, and surrender to My Ways, I can raise you to new heights. Praise and trust — these two — shape much of your future. Will you learn to praise and trust Me???"

Sept. 1

Whoever believes and is baptized will be saved.

[MARK 16:16]

"Believe and be baptized and you shall be saved. — That is only the first step — the entrance into My Kingdom and the guarantee of living eternally with Me. But then, saved from what?? Saved from **self** . . . saved from walking your own path . . . saved from disbelief . . . saved from lack of trust . . . saved from loss of hope . . . saved from false hope . . . saved from weakness . . . saved from loneliness . . . saved from **self**. . . . Step by step, as you walk with Me on this Kingdom Road, My Saving Power is available to you. Claim it! Use it!! Declare it!!! Proclaim it!!!! My Power is made perfect in human weakness. Stand firm on that promise. Walk on in My Saving Power."

Sept. 2

If God is for us, who can be against us.
We are more than conquerors through Him
Who loved us.
[ROMANS 8:31,37]

"You are a conquering force when you seek to be filled with My Spirit in your holy of holies. You are My temple. Let Me cleanse My temple with My Redeeming Fire. Yes, at times you will feel and sense that fire — burning away the **self** that dwells inside you. **Self** must die if you are to be a conquering force for My Kingdom. All evil must flee at the sound of My Name. You are My temple — all evil must flee in My Presence. Claim it! Proclaim it! Declare it! Use My Power within you to drive away all selfish thoughts. Draw near to Me. Sit at My Feet when the battles begin. Then go forth in My Power. The victory is yours."

Sept. 3

Whatever is true, whatever is noble, whatever is right, whatever is pure, whatever is lovely, whatever is admirable — if anything is excellent or praiseworthy — think about such things.
[PHILIPPIANS 4:8]

"Fix your eyes upon Me, the Author and Finisher of your faith. Fix your sight on Me. See Me at every turn. Fix your thoughts on Me. Whatever is pure and noble and right and lovely and true — think on these things. I am Pure . . . I am your Noble King of kings . . . I am Lovely . . . I am Truth . . . I am Worthy of all your praise. — Think on Me."

Sept. 4

*You will keep in perfect peace him whose mind is steadfast, because he trusts in You. Trust in the L*ORD *forever, for the L*ORD*, the L*ORD*, is the Rock eternal.*
[ISAIAH 26:3-4]

"Be still and know that I am here, awaiting you to trust Me fully at every turn, to be led by Me — in the little, as well as in the major decisions in your life . . . in your day. Come quickly to Me. Do it over and over until it becomes part of your very nature. That is the trust I desire from you — the trust you need — to walk hand in Hand with Me down life's pathways — held in My Embrace — not pulling away to go your own way."

Sept. 5

We are the clay, You are the Potter; we are all the work of Your Hand.
[ISAIAH 64:8b]

"Let Me sculpt you into a fiery gem, chipping away at the sharp edges that cause you, and others, pain. Yes, the chipping, the molding must at times be painful. But you have Me to cling to during those times of pain. And you will see the beauty of the gem reflecting My Light — radiating My Light to all those around you. As you shine for Me, the thought of that pain never again causes you grief, only joy — joy at the realization of how that pain resulted in such beauty. Shine for Me."

Sept. 6

There is now no condemnation for those who are in Christ Jesus because through Christ Jesus the law of the Spirit of Life set me free.
[ROMANS 8:1-2]

"Yes, your failures are cause for inward searching — but only to the point of brokenness and repentance. Then stop. Stop punishing yourself for past failures. Condemnation is never from Me. I came to seek and to save. Condemnation comes from the enemy. Flee from it. Those failures given to Me are forgiven . . . forgotten. Pain me not with your impulse to revisit them. Do you not trust My Forgiving Grace?? Trust Me. Trust in My Unfailing Love. Trust Me so fully that thanksgiving and praise pour forth from a thankful heart for that forgiveness and cleansing . . . never revisiting those past failures again with self-condemnation in your heart. Trust Me. My Love covers a multitude of sins. Let My Perfect Love cast out all your fears and failures. You are forgiven. You are clean. Trust Me. You are set free."

Sept. 7

You will call upon Me and come and pray to
Me, and I will listen to you.
You will seek Me and find Me when you seek
Me with all your heart.
[JEREMIAH 29:12-13]

((LORD, Thy Will be done in my life!
I seek Your Face. . . .
I seek Your Will. . . .
I seek Your Path. . . .))

"Seek, and you shall find Me, and find all the glad sur-
prises I have in store for you, as well as the stony uphill
stretches of the road ahead. But take My Hand and My
Yoke, and the burden will be only as heavy as you make it,
when you pull away, or try to run ahead of Me."

Sept. 8

He Who began a good work in you will carry it on to completion.
[PHILIPPIANS 1:6]

"Do not let the things of this world encroach on My time with you, or on you receiving My Love for you, or on your godly vision for the days ahead. Have I not told you to seek Me first? Then all else will flow out of our close-knit relationship, and your focus will be on Me and My Power. And My Peace-giving Spirit will lead you along the path I have planned for you each day. Today, be more focused on Me than you were yesterday. Be more in love with Me today. Speak to Me and hear My WORDS spoken to your heart more clearly today. Today, love and encourage and comfort others more than you could yesterday. Today, be more zealous for Me. Today, speak more kindly to others. Be more at peace. . . . And so it goes . . . making each day another step towards completion."

Sept. 9

My soul yearns for You in the night; in the morning my spirit longs for you.
[ISAIAH 26:9]

((I long for You, LORD —more of You, LORD, more and more.))

"Child, I long for your companionship. Come feast with Me at My Table of Blessings — at My Love Feast — set up just for you. In deep companionship with Me, I am those Blessings — I am that Love when you come with Me into My Inner Sanctuary. . . . My Hope, My Joy, My Peace — all available to you in this complete union with Me — hand in Hand — heart to Heart. Sit down now, child, and feast on My Presence. There is no joy, no love, no peace you have ever known that will match what you will have in this delicate union of our spirits. Come to the Feast."

Sept. 10

Come to Me, all you who are weary and
burdened, and I will give you rest.
Take My Yoke upon you and learn from Me,
for I am Gentle and Humble in Heart, and
you will find rest for your souls. For My Yoke
is easy and My burden is light.
[MATTHEW 11:28-30]

"Sit at My Feet. Throw down your burdens. Nail **self** — your will — to the cross. What remains — a yielded will — now more easily fits into My Yoke. Take My Yoke upon you so that your way is clear — led and guided by My Hand. That Yoke seems, at first, constricting and confining. But as you yield to its pressure and guidance, you see how freeing it is — how protected you are — how much freer from worry and fear you are now. Your burdens are now Mine to carry. As your will embraces My Perfect Will, you are set free. Come, child, take My Yoke upon you."

Sept. 11

I have loved you with an Everlasting Love; I have drawn you with Loving-Kindness.
[JEREMIAH 31:3]

((O LORD, all I need, all I want, is to be with You. Here I am, at Your Feet, just to be with You.))

"For you to come to Me . . . just to be with Me . . . without one plea . . . is so tender to Me. Constant companions, constant communion, constant intimacy ~~ like none other you know on this earth. Sit in silence with Me, engulfed in My Presence. Then, in the moments of your heart-cry, know that I am here with you. And the responses to your heart-cries are already awaiting those cries. Lean back in My Arms now, and find quiet assurance of My Love."

Sept. 12

*You fill me with joy in Your Presence,
with eternal pleasures at Your Right Hand.*
[PSALM 16:11]

"Wait in silence before Me. I fill you first with the Light of My Presence, and then joy floods your soul and you are held in the Palm of My Hand. Nothing can separate you from Me, from My Love — nothing but your **self**! **Self** — the root of all dissatisfaction, all discord. **Self** must die if you are to experience Me fully. **Self** separates you from Me. The enemy uses **self** to destroy peace and harmony and love. **Self** must be replaced with a humble, contrite heart that seeks Me above all else. In My Presence is safety; and fullness of joy springs forth from a heart that is touched by My Love, My Forgiveness, My Grace, My Mercy. Come into My Presence. . . .You will be changed."

Sept. 13

I call on the LORD in My distress and He answers me.
[PSALM 120:1]

"Lean on Me when the battles are raging. My Strength is made perfect in your weakness. Use My Power that is mighty to the pulling down of strongholds that imprison you and those you love. Use My Power to bring Peace and Joy and Strength and health. Then will My Name be glorified — My Power displayed. Use that Power. Use it, and in turn you will be strengthened — strengthened in spirit . . . in life. Use it, and you will witness My Love conquering all your fears. Use it, and you will see the lost turn around and follow Me. Use it, and you will fortify My Church. Use it for My Glory. Use it."

Sept. 14

Set your mind on things above.
And live a life of love.
[COLOSSIANS 3:2a]
[EPHESIANS 5:2a]

"You are My conduit of My Love, My Mercy and Grace, My Comfort and Loving-Kindness — when you keep your mind and your spirit fixed on Me, and have the mind of Christ — and My Spirit living and active inside you to empower you. You can do nothing apart from Me that impacts My Kingdom for the good of My People, for the saving of the lost among you. Instead, reach out and touch them with My Power, My Love, My Grace, My WORDS."

Sept. 15

I made you grow like a plant of the field.
You grew up and developed and became the
most beautiful of jewels.
[EZEKIEL 16:7]

"In My Hands, you are a delicate flower, reaching your face to the Son, absorbing My Light, producing a sweet fragrance — drawing others to Me. Be fed by the Vine. Do not let anyone or anything pluck you from the Vine. There, it is, you are fed by My Life Flow, watered by My Love."

Sept. 16

For the WORD *of the* LORD *is right and true;*
He is faithful in all He does.
[PSALM 33:4]

"I am your God Eternal — your Friend . . . your Healer
. . . your Lover. And, yet, I am your King, your Savior,
your Master, your Protector and your Guide. Seek Me in
all these roles. When you need a healer of disease — a
healer of your broken heart — I am right here beside you
to hold you close to My Heart. When you need and want
a Protector, a Savior from this dark world, a Friend — I
am here. I hold you in the Palm of My Hand, and lead
you in the way you should go. When you bow to Me as
LORD and Master, as King over your heart and soul, I am
here to raise My Banner of Love over you, and claim you
as one of My own — as a Levite to go before My army
in worship and song — or as a foot soldier to do battle
with the enemy — or as an intercessory prayer warrior. —
Whatever I call you to do, I am here for you."

Sept. 17

Yield your hearts to the LORD.
[JOSHUA 24:23b]

"I am your Compassionate, Gracious God, Who Loves you more than you can know. I want ALL of you — your whole being — heart, mind, body, soul, spirit. When you give yourself unreservedly to Me, I can use you to touch the hurting, the lonely, the lowly, the lost. Open your heart to Me first — then to them. You honor and glorify Me in so doing. Be at rest in My Loving Arms, giving yourself in total surrender to My Will — not begrudgingly, but willingly, with great zeal. Then, and only then, will you experience full Joy, Peace, and Love. Go forth now, under My Banner of Love."

Sept. 18

Serve Him with wholehearted devotion and with a willing mind, for the LORD searches every heart and understands the motive behind the thoughts.
[1 CHRONICLES 28:9]

"I yearn for your tender acts of loving devotion to Me — to each other. What Joy and Comfort flood My Heart when you turn to Me with praise, and love, and a true desire to know Me on a deeper, more intimate plane. That tender desire for My Presence, for My Will to reign in your life, brings Comfort and Joy to My heart."

Sept. 19

*The LORD delights in those who fear Him,
who put their hope in His unfailing Love.*
[PSALM 147:11]

"You bring Me Joy when your heart is set apart for Me —
totally focused on Me, with no distraction of the worldly
passions knocking on your heart. Focus solely on Me. —
And bring Me Joy and Love, as you were designed for."

Sept. 20

Yours, O LORD, is the Greatness and the Power and the Glory and the Majesty and the Splendor, for everything in heaven and earth is Yours. Yours, O LORD, is the Kingdom; You are exalted as Head over all.
[1 CHRONICLES 29:11]

"Behold the Beauty of My Majesty. Where My Kingdom has been established in your life, there My Majesty reigns. Exalt Me as Head over every aspect of your life. Where you see unrest, look to Me for Peace. Trade your weakness for My Strength and My Power. Trade your fears for My Peace . . . your failure for My Forgiveness . . . your idols for My Holiness . . . your lack for My Bountiful Supply . . . your pain for My Comforting Love . . . your critical nature for My Loving-Kindness . . . your anger for My Peace . . . your unrest for My Assurance . . . your _____ for My _____. Trust Me, child, for all of these. I love you, and I want My Kingdom established in your life. Seek My Rule over every aspect of your life. Seek Me, and all of this will be fulfilled. Trust Me, child, to meet you at the point of your need. Seek Me, and you will find Me waiting to display My Majesty."

Sept. 21

I will praise you, O LORD, with all my heart;
I will tell of all your wonders.
[PSALM 9:1]

"Praise! — Praise! — Praise! — All evil must flee! Give your life to Me. Live your life for Me. Declare My Goodness, My Mercy, My Love — even in the pain — **especially** in the pain. Focus your attention on Me and you will be set free from the pain. Praise Me. Tell of My wonderful Love and Mercy, and then My Power will rush through you and send the enemy fleeing. Praise Me more and more."

Sept. 22

There is now no condemnation for those who are in Christ Jesus.
[ROMANS 8:1]

"Condemnation is never My Voice. Conviction — accompanied with Grace and Mercy and Love — yes. But never condemnation — not for those who love Me and serve Me wholeheartedly. Condemnation comes only from the mouth of the deceiver himself — the father of lies, who said to Eve, 'Did God really say. . .?' But there is now no condemnation for you who love and serve Me. I speak only the Truth in Love to you. Listen only to My Voice — the Voice of Truth."

Sept. 23

There is no one righteous, not even one; . . .
no one who seeks God.
All have turned away, they have together
become worthless.
[ROMANS 3:10-12]

"In My Eyes, though, you are never worthless when you submit to My Will. When you seek My Will, you are My treasure, and I can use you to the fullest. I am the Creator of the universe. And yet, I am the Creator of Saving Grace, of Life Everlasting, of your tender heart, of Joy and Love. Bask in My Love, and you will be empowered."

Sept. 24

We rejoice in our sufferings, because we know that suffering produces perseverance; perseverance, character; and character, hope. And hope does not disappoint us, because God has poured out His Love into our hearts by the Holy Spirit, Whom He has given us.
[ROMANS 5:3-5]

"As you walk through the dessert in pain and suffering, My Joy may be unreachable right then. But take courage. My Hand will strengthen you as you persevere, and you draw nearer and nearer to Me. And you will then begin to fly on wings like eagles — soaring to greater heights than you have ever experienced — as you nestle into My Arms of Love, and know our loving Friendship is being deepened and strengthened. Then My Joy will flood your heart and overflow onto others as you serve Me quietly. And you will again be filled with songs of deliverance, which too, will fill you with Joy. Walk on, knowing the best is yet to come."

Sept. 25

I stand in awe of Your deeds, O LORD.
Renew them in our day.
[HABAKKUK 3:2]

"Wait and you will see My Hand at work in the Body of Christ — among My people throughout the world — including your corner of the world. Watch, wait, and see My Glory displayed among you. You will be touched with My Power yet unknown to you. You will experience manifestations of My Spirit at work in ways you have yet to experience. Watch, wait, and see My deeds renewed and displayed in your midst."

Sept. 26

Do everything in Love.
[1 CORINTHIANS 16:14]

"Everyone — young and old — everyone needs compassion and kindness and love. When you touch others with love and compassion and kindness, you are touching them as if by Me. Be My Hands, My Eyes of Love and Compassion, My Touch of Kindness. Do everything in Love, and all you do will have lasting impact."

Sept. 27

But as for me, it is good to be near God.
[PSALM 73:28a]

"Spend your days with Me ~~ embraced by My Love ~~ comforted and cleansed by My WORD ~~ empowered by My Spirit ~~ by My Love. Come away with Me into My Holy of Holies. Join Me in sweet communion. Know that I am always here for you, waiting to reveal more of Myself to you. Come to Me."

Sept. 28

You will receive Power when the Holy Spirit comes on you.
[ACTS 1:8a]

"The Power of My Spirit is at your disposal. Use it! Claim it! Release it! Never fail to use it when you are under attack! My Power conquers — making you the victor. Use it constantly. Now rest in Me. — Rest in My Arms of Love. Go forth in My Power. Claim and declare My Victory."

Sept. 29

Be sure to fear the LORD and serve Him faithfully with all your heart; consider what great things He has done for you.
[1 SAMUEL 12:24]

"I need your help and the help of others in My Kingdom, to touch the hearts of men — human-to-human. My Supernatural Touch then flows through you. With many people, and for many circumstances, only a human touch will do the work needed at that moment. Understand this Truth, and you will grasp how much I need My people to have a servant's heart — to serve Me out of reverent awe of Me, yes — but also out of our intimate Friendship. Dearest friends will do anything for each other — selflessly ministering to their friend's needs. Do likewise for Me — as I do for you. It is with great Love for you, that I provide for your every need, that I am here for you. What joy and honor you bring to Me when you do likewise. Be available. Be used. Be rewarded with a more loving and intimate tie with Me. I Love you so dearly."

Sept. 30

*I will forgive their wickedness and will
remember their sins no more.*
[HEBREWS 8:12]

Remember not the sins of my youth.
[PSALM 25:7]

*I am He Who blots out your transgressions,
for My Own Sake, and remembers your sins
no more.*
[ISAIAH 43:25]

"I remember no confessed sin. You mustn't either. To hold onto those sins by re-visiting them — even with remorse — adds to My Sorrows. I forgave you — you must forgive yourself and never look back. My Love, and My Blood, cover over and wash away those sins, and replace them with My Righteousness that I have clothed you with. All darkness is washed away and hidden. Forgive yourself. Be set free from the bondage. Put on My Robe of Righteousness. Walk away from that old darkness into My Marvelous Light. Come with Me in the shadow of My Wings — clean and forgiven."

Oct. 1

Do nothing out of selfish ambition . . . Your attitude should be the same as that of Christ Jesus: Who made Himself nothing, taking the very nature of a servant.

[PHILIPPIANS 2:3,5,7]

"When your spirit, soul, and body are fully dedicated to Me — desiring only My Will for your life, for your days — you act as My conduit — an open channel for My Love, My Peace, My Healing Power, My Joy. . . . **Self** must die! — If it does not die, it blocks that channel so My Spirit is not free to flow through you. Choose this day which way it shall be — a selfish lifestyle, or an unblocked channel through which My Spirit flows, touching and changing you and those you love and care about. So choose."

Oct. 2

You are a chosen people, a royal priesthood,
a holy nation, a people belonging to God,
that you may declare the praises of Him Who
called you out of darkness
into His wonderful Light.
[1 PETER 2:9]

"Look to Me for full forgiveness — never dwelling on past failures. The shame is washed away by My Blood. Hold not onto past shame. That drives the nails deeper into My Hands. Be clean. Live now with a fresh start daily. Each morning, rise with a new realization of who you are in Me, who you are to Me. You are My child. You are a royal priest in My Kingdom of Light. I have called you out of darkness. Leave that darkness behind. I give you now the weapon of praise, to vanquish that darkness. Use it for My Glory."

Oct. 3

You are my Lamp, O LORD; the LORD turns my darkness into Light.
[2 SAMUEL 22:29]

"Daily search within, to find the deep places within you that need My touch — My Healing Power. Hear My WORDS of conviction. Listen not to the condemning lies of the enemy. I call you up to a higher, purer nature. He seeks to tear down and destroy you. Hear My tender Voice calling you out of darkness, into My Marvelous Light — each day, drawing you closer and closer to Me. Take heart, though, child, as I reveal what you need to let go of, or what needs to be changed in your life, in your heart. Just know that the closer you get to the Light, the more you see the darkness within you. You never know darkness until your heart is drawn close to Mine and to My Marvelous Light. That is the secret of My Kingdom that only those few who seek My ever-increasing nearness ever know. Open up the hidden doors within your heart which hide that darkness. I stand at those doors and knock."

Oct. 4

*Suffering produces perseverance;
perseverance, character; and character,
hope.
And hope does not disappoint us, because
God has poured out His Love into our hearts
by the Holy Spirit, Whom He has given us.*
[ROMANS 5:3b-5]

*This happened that we might not rely on
ourselves but on God.*
[2 CORINTHIANS 1:9]

"It is out of My Love for you that I allow you to suffer pain — pain that draws you closer to Me — pain that ceases activities that have drawn you away from Me. Suffering produces lasting strength of character that cannot be learned any other way. Character produces Hope, and Hope does not disappoint you, because it increases your dependence on Me and your love for Me. Life with Me will not disappoint you."

Oct. 5

*Above all, love each other deeply, because
love covers over a multitude of sins.*
[1 PETER 4:8]

"Treat all as you would treat Me — with love and consideration and kindness. Let nothing others do to you alter your treatment of them. I was spat upon and mocked and flogged, and yet, I prayed, 'Father, forgive them.' Out of a heart of Love, I prayed for them. You, too, must pray for your oppressors. And pray for your own strength, and for a peaceful spirit, and a heart of compassion. In order to bring Me praise, accept one another, just as I accept you."

Oct. 6

LORD, You establish Peace for us; all that we have accomplished You have done for us.
[ISAIAH 26:12]

"You are My conduit of My Power through the work of My Spirit when you leave an open channel for Me — unblocked by fear, unblocked by self, by pride. Call on My Perfect Love that will cast out all those fears. And it is by My Grace that you have been saved — saved from sin, yes, but able also to be saved from fear, from self, from pride, from all worldly influence, when you walk in freedom, by claiming My Grace and My Power. Claim it, use it, declare it. Let go of those hindering spirits and loose My Power, My Authority, My Kingdom into each life, each heart, each relationship, each home that you pray for and touch — led by My Spirit — My Loving Spirit."

Oct. 7

Your Hand will guide me, Your Right Hand will hold me fast.
[PSALM 139:10]

"Leave it all in My Hands — every fear, every failure, every burden — every faded joy, every sin, every crisis — every battle, every victory lost — every choice, every decision — every moment, every day. Leave it all in My Hands. Then take My Hand and follow Me. You will see wonders unfold."

Oct. 8

Jesus went out as usual to the Mount of Olives. On reaching that place, He knelt down and prayed.
[LUKE 22:39a,40a,41b]

"Being out here with Me in the great outdoors is like when I would go to solitary places upon a mountainside to get away from the multitudes to pray and just soak up the Love and Companionship of My Father. Nature is My treatment, My nurse, for tired and weary bodies, tired and weary souls. Sit in My Arms and let My Healing Balm wash over you. You are Mine. You are cleansed. You are forgiven. You are set free. Go in Peace."

Oct. 9

As for me, I am filled with Power with the Spirit of the LORD.

[MICAH 3:8a]

"I am right beside you — in sickness and in health — in poverty and in wealth — in your days of sorrow and your days of Joy. I am your Strength, your Joy. Dwell with Me and be filled with My Power. I am your Strength, your Joy, your Source of all that satisfies that inner hunger. Absorb My Food for your soul, your spirit, your thoughts. Come along beside Me — hand in Hand. Be upheld and stabilized and balanced. I am the balance in your life. I stabilize your stumbling heart. Be filled with My Power to stabilize your wandering spirit, your wandering heart. I am your source of Power. Think on that. Never dwell on your weaknesses and failures. When you are at your weakest, that is when I can — and I will — show Myself Strong. Call on the Power of My Spirit to fill you, to empower you, to do My Will. Let Me then lead you into all Truth, and satisfy your desires with good things, which I will provide in due time. You are washed clean with My Blood. My Banner over you is Love. Condemnation comes only from the enemy — to keep you from Me — to keep you from My mission for your life. Put on your full armor. Stand firm. Walk hand in Hand with Me. Go forth unafraid, filled with My Power."

Oct. 10

*The LORD is my rock, my fortress
and my deliverer;
my God is my rock, in Whom I take refuge,
my shield and the horn of my salvation.
He is my stronghold, my refuge and my
Savior.
I call to the LORD, Who is worthy of praise,
and I am saved from my enemies.*
[2 SAMUEL 22:2-4]

"I am your Refuge in times of trouble — a Refuge from stress, from busy-ness, from fear, from pain, from depression, from being brokenhearted. Praise will also send those evils and distress fleeing. Come into My Sanctuary — My place of refuge — My Presence. You will be safe — you will be changed — you will be set free. Sit a while with Me under the shelter of My Wings. Here you are totally safe — totally Mine — totally set free."

Oct. 11

You will fill me with joy in Your Presence.
[PSALM 16:11b] / [ACTS 2:28b]

"My Heart — Seek after My Heart. Dwell in the presence of My Unfailing Love and Joy. Seek after My Touch — My tender Touch. I love you. I will not fail you. I will never leave you to face life on your own. Dwell daily in My Presence. Come into the Secret Place of the Most High. There, even in toughest of times, you will find Peace, Love, Rest, even Joy, when you focus solely on Me, and the sweetness of My Presence, My Love."

Oct. 12

I stand in awe of Your Deeds, O LORD.
Renew them in our day.
[HABAKKUK 3:2]

"I long to manifest My Power in the body of Christ. But there are still so few who appropriate My Power in their lives ~~ in their gatherings ~~ due to lack of faith, lack of vision, lack of love for Me. The deeper your love for Me, the deeper your faith in Me, the more My Work will be displayed in your midst, in your lives. You will indeed stand in awe at the Work of My Hands."

Oct. 13

For God, who said, "Let light shine out of darkness," made His Light shine in our hearts to give us the Light of the knowledge of the Glory of God in the Face of Christ.
[2 CORINTHIANS 4:6]

"Into the darkness and into the gloom, I shine My Light, and reveal the Beauty of My Kingdom in contrast to all the evil that lurks in the darkness. And I shine My Light into the shadows in your heart to make all things bright and beautiful within you. And now you are called to let My Light shine through you — into the lives of those around you. Be a beacon of Light showing the world the brightness they are so desperately in search of in their dark lives."

Oct. 14

Give and it will be given to you.
A good measure, pressed down,
shaken together and running over will be
poured into your lap.
[LUKE 6:38]

"Your first desire should be to give of yourself — your heart, your life, your love, your devotion, your gifting. You will be astounded at the number of hearts you can touch — the number of hearts you can fill. Unconditional love — Agape Love — My Love that I desire for you to exhibit, requires nothing in return. — Nothing from Me . . . nothing from those you touch. But My promise will be fulfilled. You will receive a good measure of My Love, My Touch, My Blessings, My Presence. So give, and it will be given to you. I promise."

Oct. 15

Therefore I tell you, do not worry about your life.
Who of you by worrying can add a single hour to his life?
[MATTHEW 6:25a,27]

"You cannot have worry or anxiety, or anxious thoughts, when My Presence surrounds you. My Presence causes all evil to flee. When anxious thoughts fill your soul, come quickly into My Presence, and you will find rest for your soul. You will trust Me more deeply each time you follow through on this and seek My Presence and My Arms to hold you. Trust is the underlying freedom from anxiety and anxious thoughts and fears. So trust Me more and more. My Love, My Presence is surrounding you, even now. Trust Me, love Me, more and more."

Oct. 16

*Praise be to the God and Father of our LORD
Jesus Christ, the Father of Compassion and
the God of all Comfort, Who comforts us in
all our troubles, so that we can comfort
those in any trouble with the comfort we
ourselves have received from God.
For just as the sufferings of Christ flow over
into our lives,
so also through Christ our comfort overflows.*
[2 CORINTHIANS 1:3-5]

"The suffering you have been through gives you compassion for My hurting world. It heightens your gift of mercy and encouragement for others. Use it for My Glory. Fix your eyes on Me and in so doing, see My Gentle Touch on you and on the pain you have been through, drawing you closer and closer to Me. See how I have and will continue to work all those sufferings for your good and the good of those who cross your path. Never doubt Me. Never doubt My Power to seek and to save those who are lost in sin, in fear, in doubt, in self. Go after them with Me. Use your gift to love them into My Kingdom. Nothing draws them more strongly than My Forgiving Unconditional Love. Be a channel of that Love."

Oct. 17

*O LORD, You have searched me and
You know me.
Search me, O God, and know my heart;
test me and know my anxious thoughts.*
[PSALM 139:1,23]

*My son, do not despise the LORD's discipline
and do not resent His rebuke,
because the LORD disciplines those He loves,
as a father the son he delights in.*
[PROVERBS 3:11,12]

"Check yourself. Search out your own heart. If there be any wicked, selfish, childish, hateful, anxious, complacent, worldly way in you, repent of it. And I will set you free from it. If you do not, I will search you, and, as a father disciplines his son, I will discipline you, and give you lessons in your life to teach you, and bring you to repentance. . . . You choose the path."

Oct. 18

Perfect Love drives out fear,
because fear has to do with punishment.
[1 JOHN 4:18]

"Hunger after Me. Hunger and thirst no more of the lustful and worldly things. Your old nature was hung on the cross with Me. Satan was bound. You were set free — set free to love Me above all else — to desire My Presence above all. Sit and wait in My Presence until your soul is tightly enwrapped by My Perfect Love that casts away all your fears."

Oct. 19

Show the wonder of Your great Love.
[PSALM 17:7a]

"My Love is what sustains you, what gives you Life and Peace and Strength. It is My Love that binds My people together in perfect unity. Where that unity is lacking, My Love has not been sought, or allowed to enwrap them. Where My Love is squelched, My people suffer and die. My Church can only flourish and do My Will if My Love is allowed to flow freely. Each of My children must be a channel of the outpouring of that Love."

Oct. 20

Let us fix our thoughts on Jesus.
[HEBREWS 12:2a]

"No matter what occupies your hands, turn your thoughts, your eyes, your ears to Me. Fix your eyes on Me, and you will gain the victory. Call to Me; seek My Face and My Ways. You will be victorious. Commune with Me. Sing to Me. Find Joy and Peace in My Presence. All else will fade."

Oct. 21

Jesus said, "Peace be with you! As the Father has sent Me, I am sending you." And with that, He breathed on them and said, "Receive the Holy Spirit."
[JOHN 20:21-22]

"You are precious in My sight because I love you. I created you, breathed Life into you — both as you were being birthed by your mother — and again, when I recreated you and sent My Spirit to live inside you, and then again to empower you. I breathe Life into you each time you call on Me to show My Power in your life. I breathe Life into your very being, to empower you to do My Will. Breathe in deeply this Life flow. My Breath of Life empowers you."

Oct. 22

*Acknowledge the God of your father, and
serve Him with wholehearted devotion and
with a willing mind, for the LORD searches
every heart and understands every motive
behind the thoughts.*
[1 CHRONICLES 28:9]

"What I desire of you is pure devotion to Me, and to My Will for you. . . . Pure devotion is not grudgingly saying, 'I have to?!?!? OKAY then.' . . . But it is the deep desire of a heart filled with Love for Me — a heart eager to embrace My Will, and honor Me. From that embrace, comes the anticipation of what each moment of the day will bring . . . so that the interruptions, the unexpected happenings of the day, can be viewed from this perspective — that it is all in My Hands, awaiting your eager turning to Me for direction, for strength, for guidance. Be ready, be willing, be fully devoted to Me out of a pure loving heart."

Oct. 23

Therefore, holy brothers, who share in the heavenly calling, fix your thoughts on Jesus.
[HEBREWS 3:1]

"Your life, set apart with Me. — Make it the all-consuming part of your day. Sit with Me, walk with Me, serve Me, seek Me, rest in My Arms. . . .Fix your eyes on Me — fix your thoughts on Me. . . . Go where I lead you. Do as I would do."

Oct. 24

Commit your way to the LORD; trust in Him
and
He will do this:
He will make your righteousness
shine like the dawn.
[PSALM 37:5-6a]

"Be a beacon of My Light and Love. Shine on all those I bring into your path, drawing them to Me. By your actions, your life, your love, they will be more attracted to Me, than by the oracle of scholars. They must see Me in action through you. Lovingly serve them. Do unto others as I have done unto you."

Oct. 25

The same Lord is Lord of all and richly blesses all who call on Him, for, "Everyone who calls on the Name of the Lord will be saved."
[ROMANS 10:12b-13 / JOEL 2:32a]

I am with you and will watch over you wherever you go.
[GENESIS 28:15a]

"Call out My Name and I am there — there to comfort . . . to calm . . . to provide . . . to bless . . . to nurture . . . to nourish you — with My Love . . . My Provision . . . My Presence . . . My Security . . . My Life . . . My Love."

Oct. 26

*Satisfy us in the morning with
Your unfailing Love,
that we may sing for joy and be glad
all our days.*
[PSALM 90:14]

"JOY!! Take JOY when you serve those around you. It is in service — in being the least of them — that you are truly lifted to great heights within you. Feel that JOY rise within you. When you pour out My Love onto others, there is no greater service to be done. I came to give Life and to give it more abundantly. Live that Abundant Life when you pour out My Love, My Life, My JOY into the lives — and into the hearts — of those I bring into your path. Walk with Me along that path and you will dwell in the Secret Place of the Most High. Pass those Royal Treasures onto the hurting, the needy, the joyous, the strong. — Each one is in need of more of Me."

Oct. 27

Great is Your Love toward me.
You, O LORD, are a Compassionate
and Gracious God,
abounding in Love and Faithfulness.
[PSALM 86:13,15]

"You are the object of My Love and Compassion when you cry to Me out of despair, fear, or helplessness, yes! But also when you cry to Me with thanksgiving and praise from your heart, out of your love for Me. Whether in great need ~~ or overflowing with joy, with love, with thanksgiving ~~ I am always here to hold you in My Arms of Love and Security. I long to shower you with My Love and Compassion. Come to Me ~~ moment by moment ~~ come to Me. I am here for you ~~ now and always."

Oct. 28

The LORD watches over all who love Him.
[PSALM 145:20a]

"I hear your every plea — whether it is a big, or a small trial you are facing. I am right there watching over you. Your cry to Me, out of your love for Me, out of your trust in My Promised Love for you, reaches up to Me as sweet incense. Link your heart to Mine. Our communion seals all My Promises to you."

Oct. 29

I will listen to what God the LORD will say;
He promises Peace to His people.
[PSALM 85:8]

"Keep your ears attuned to My Voice. Even in the darkest, loudest corner, you can hear My Still Small Voice. Listen, child, and you shall hear My Whispers to your heart. When you sense My Presence, then Peace and Joy will surge through your very being. And you will walk with courage and strength."

Oct. 30

I am the Way and the Truth and the Life.
No one comes to the Father, except through
Me.
[JOHN 14:6]

"A life fully consecrated to Me alone is My desire of you. Live your life as unto Me. Seek Me first and foremost, to order your day aright. I am the Way — the Way to My Father's Loving Arms — the Way to Strength and survival — the Way to Love, Liberty, Freedom. I am the Truth — the Truth to base your life upon — the Truth for every decision. I am the Life — the Life that gives you life — Abundant Life — a rich, full, enduring life set apart totally to Me."

Oct. 31

You were taught, with regard to your former way of life, to put off your old self, which is being corrupted by its deceitful desires; to be made new in the attitude of your minds; and to put on the new self, created to be like God in true righteousness and holiness.
[EPHESIANS 4:22-24]

"There is only one thing that separates you from Me — self — that old prideful, sinful self. And when selfish pride steps up, that is when you are so easily hurt by others. Is it a contest to see which of you can be more selfish? Is it really more blessed to assert prideful self, than to give yourself in service and sacrifice to Me? — To give truly selfless love to each other? . . . Think on these things. . . .

A life — emptied of self — a life given in service to Me — a life fully consecrated to Me — a life pouring out My Unconditional Love onto others. . . . No greater Joy. . . . No greater reward. . . . Think on these things."

Nov. 1

*Now that I, your Lord and Teacher,
have washed your feet,
you also should wash one another's feet.*
[JOHN 13:14-15]

"You are called to a special purpose — designed for only you to fulfill. Each day that purpose may change. Today that purpose might be, 'Love that certain neighbor as yourself.' Tomorrow it might be, 'Wash her feet.' So, shod your feet with readiness to do My bidding each day. Joy will be your reward."

Nov. 2

But as for me, it is good to be near God.
[PSALM 73:28a]

"Sensing My Spirit is to know I am near. Live in that nearness, with My Spirit filling every corner of your being — no closets untouched. Sense the flow of My Spirit pulsing through your soul, searching each secret spot. Give yourself totally to My Touch."

Nov. 3

My eyes are fixed on You, O Sovereign LORD.
[PSALM 141:8a]

You have given me wisdom and power;
You have made known to me
what we asked of You.
[DANIEL 2:23]

"I will give you wisdom and strength to do My Calling on your life each day. Ask for My Will to be completed in you today. Apart from Me, you can do nothing of lasting value. Be kind and compassionate to those around you, who have yet to reach the perfection you want of them. You have been there. And even now, you recognize some of the darkness yet to be changed into light in your own heart, in your own life. Come to Me and let Me carry you through life's storms, which that darkness brings. Then be My Arms to carry others through their storms. Do not add weight to their already heavy heart, and make them sink and drown. Instead, lift them up out of the deep water they have entered. Be My Saving Arms."

Nov. 4

Do everything in love.
[1 CORINTHIANS 16:14]

"Whatever you do, do it out of love for Me; do it out of love for others, as I have loved you. Do nothing out of vain conceit. You are not serving to gain recognition if you are truly serving Me and being My representative. You are serving out of a pure heart when you serve as unto Me, and when you act and respond out of love — My Love. You are Mine — Mine to call into service, to bring My Kingdom to earth as it is in Heaven. You are Mine. Do everything in love."

Nov. 5

When I said, "My foot is slipping," Your Love,
O LORD, supported me.
When anxiety was great within me, Your
Consolation brought Joy to my soul.
[PSALM 94:18,19]

"Your praise opens the flood gates of Heaven. Joy and Peace, Strength and Love come rushing in to cover you and carry you through this season. Joy — Joy is not unreachable. — Quite the opposite! Even in the darkest times and seasons, Joy is right there within your grasp. Take hold of it by reaching out to those around you. How can you touch them in their need? Service to others, loving on others, nurturing a needy child, sharing My Life and My Love and My WORD with the hurting, but stopping first to look to Me with praise in your heart, will bring you joy. That may seem impossible in those darkest depressions of life. . . . But find even one thing to praise Me for — My Love . . . your forgiveness . . . ways I have been there for you in the past. . . . Where would you be now had I not had mercy on you at that moment in time? . . . Know that you are cherished. . . . You are loved. . . . You are treasured by the Most High God of the universe. . . . You are Mine. Take hold of Me on a deeper level than ever before. Then Joy will flood your heart."

Nov. 6

If God is for us, who can be against us?
We are more than conquerors through
Him Who loved us.
[ROMANS 8:31b,37]

"My Conquering Power — Claim it!! Use it!! You will never be denied it, if you proclaim it. Be strong and take courage. I am standing with you. I set up a standard against the enemy when I paid your price on the cross and rose again to New Life. You must rise again to New Life and be more than a conqueror — as the weapons of your warfare are not carnal, but are mighty to the breaking down of strongholds, and crushing the enemy with My Conquering Power. Use it! Claim it! Live victoriously from here on!! My Power is with you. Use it!"

Nov. 7

You fill me with joy in Your Presence.
[ACTS 2:28b]

"Come and sit with Me in My Inner Chamber. That is your sole source of My Life, My Strength, and My Love. There, too, you will find the freedom of heart and spirit, to serve Me by pouring out My Mercy, My Grace, My Love on those I put in your path. Go out in My Strength. Take courage. All is well. You are My child, My servant, My friend. ~~ Friend of God ~~ Think on that. . . . A friend loves at all times. Love and be loved. Your True Friend is He Who never leaves you nor forsakes you. Your True Friend is He Who gave His Life for you, willingly, lovingly. And then lovingly, I come to prepare a place for you ~~ no not just in heaven, but here in My Inner Chamber. So come, sit here with Me and soak in My Love. As you bask in My Presence, all fear must flea, all unrest be gone. Peace now fills those empty chambers in your inner-most being. Sense My Presence washing you clean and filling you with My Love. Never miss these times of preparation. Empty, you fail. But filled with My Power, there is no limit to how I can use you. Go forth unafraid. I am with you to lead you and guide you in My Ways. I love you, child. Go forth unafraid. My Perfect Love casts out all those fears. Come into My Secret Place, moment by moment. There, in My Secret Place, is where you will find that inner strength to carry on My Mission for your life. Seek Me 1st and then, all this will be added unto you."

Nov. 8

The LORD confides in those who fear Him.
[PSALM 25:14a]

Be still, and know that I am God.
[PSALM 46:10a]

"Yes, child, I would speak this way to My multitudes, but there are so few with listening ears. Hurry is the worst enemy of listening ears. Hurry here; hurry there. . . . Leaves little time to sit in silence before Me. Time with Me cannot be rushed, for that destroys your perfect peace within. Abide with Me. ABIDE. . . . Peace. . . . Be still. . . . Be still and know that I am God. ABIDE! "

Nov. 9

But as for me, I am filled with Power, with the Spirit of the Lord.
[MICAH 3:8a]

"You so often do not live as though you are filled with My Power. Think of it, the Power that raised the Son — the Messiah — from the dead, is available to you — just by the asking. Appropriate My Power not only in your weakness, not only as an intercessor, but in your day-to-day walk. When you walk under My yoke, having dropped your burdens at My Feet, and walking in that Power of the Living God, no weapon formed against you can prosper or cause you despair. In this world you will have tribulation but I have overcome the evil in this world by that same Power of My Spirit. Ask and you shall receive that very Power."

Nov. 10

*When I am afraid, I will trust in You.
In God, Whose WORD I praise, in God I trust;
I will not be afraid.*
[PSALM 56:3-4a]

"Change your fears to praise as you trust Me fully. Never let your fears keep you from loving Me — trusting Me — and praising Me for My Abundant Goodness to you. Sing with praise and thanksgiving — and those fears must flee. Standing in My Holy Presence must bring you to your knees, in reverent awe. Seek Me first when those fears assail you. My Perfect Love must cast out those fears, and set you free to love Me again. Fear and Love cannot co-exist."

Nov. 11

My soul finds rest in God alone; my hope
comes from Him.
Trust in Him, at all times, O people; pour out
your hearts to Him.
[PSALM 62:1a,5b,8]

"Remember, child, My Heart's desire is to be in constant communion with you. Talk to Me, your Dearest Friend, moment-by-moment as the day wears on. Come to Me with needs, yes, but come to Me, just to be in communion with Me — sharing your intimate thoughts, thanksgivings, and praise — along with your cries for help. When you are weakest — for whatever reason — I am Strongest — in whatever way you need strength — Mighty, Powerful Warrior . . . Tender-hearted God of Compassion . . . Gentle, Forgiving Friend. Come to Me, not only when you are weary."

Nov. 12

You will be made rich in every way so that you can be generous on every occasion, and your generosity . . . will result in thanksgiving to God.
[2 CORINTHIANS 9:11]

"The gifts you receive from Me — both physical gifts and spiritual gifts — are meant to be used in My Kingdom, and for the expanding of My Kingdom — on earth as it is in heaven. Decades ago, My Kingdom would have been established here on earth, if only My gifts had been used for My Glory. Start today. What have I given to you that you can give away . . . or use to build My Kingdom?"

Nov. 13

The LORD gave and the LORD has taken away; may the Name of the LORD be praised. Shall we accept good from God, and not trouble?

[JOB 1:21b; 2:10b]

"What seems like good, and plenty, may actually lead to your downfall. Therefore taking away much of that which seemed good to you, will then actually lead to deeper fulfillment, and richer, more abundant life. Thus, praise Me in the deepest valley, the most violent storm, and you will gain deepest fulfillment. You will come to know that your most precious treasures are not your earthly 'treasures,' but are the pearls of wisdom; pearls of strength in times of peril; pearls of joy, unknown to those caught up in worldly pleasures; the treasure of peace which passes all understanding; of fulfillment in knowing you are treasured by the Most High God; and the most precious treasure of the purest, sweetest, dearest relationship with Jesus — your One True Friend who knows you deeply, loves you purely, cherishes you dearly, supports you fully, listens to your heart cries — your constant Companion, Lover, and Friend. — The truest Treasure ever known to man."

Nov. 14

"Even now," declares the LORD,
"return to Me with all your heart, with
fasting
and weeping and mourning."
Rend your heart. . . . Return to the LORD your
God, for He is gracious and compassionate,
slow to anger and abounding in love.
[JOEL 2:12-13]

"When you are led astray by worldly passions, come to Me wholeheartedly, expectantly and humbly. Declare a fast — a fast from those earthly pleasures that lured you away from Me. As you continue in that fast, those earthly desires will be weakened more and more — so much so, that they will become distasteful to you, and you will spew them out of your mouth, out of your sight. That is when you can draw nearer to Me out of a reverent, consecrated heart. Then it is that you will seek My Face and set your desires on Me — above all else. Repent of your sinful ways and return to Me — to My Loving Arms held out to you, awaiting your arrival. Rend your heart — return to Me."

Nov. 15

I stand in awe of Your deeds, O Lord.
Renew them in our day,
in our time make them known.
[HABAKKUK 3:2]

Show the wonder of Your Great Love.
[PSALM 17:7a]

"I wait, watching to find the lost, the lonely, the hurting, and yet, the searching hearts. That is when My Deeds display the great wonder of My Love. Come to Me not only when your burden is heavy, not only when your soul needs to find rest. Come to Me as a little child comes to his mother's waiting arms, crawls into her lap, and is wrapped in her love. So you too, child, come to your Father's waiting Arms. Be enwrapped in My Love. Be lavished with My deeds of Mercy and My deeds of Grace."

Nov. 16

*You are my LORD; apart from You I
have no good thing.*
[PSALM 16:2]

"I am Good. All good things come from Me. At first they may not always appear to be good, as you have seen. But I am He Who brings good out of sorrow and weeping. I am He Who brings good out of weakness. I am He Who brings good out of illness and pain. — I am He Who brings you good. Trust Me in this."

Nov. 17

He said to me, "My Grace is sufficient for you, for My Power is made perfect in weakness." Therefore, I will boast all the more gladly about my weaknesses, so that Christ's Power may rest on me. . . . For when I am weak, then I am strong.
[2 CORINTHIANS 12:9-10]

"When you are weakest, I am strongest. Lean on My Strength. Call it forth, and watch My Power at work in your life — in the lives of those you bring before Me. When they are weak, My Power will be displayed in their lives as a testimony to My Greatness. Wait with patience. My Wonders never cease. Out of faith, appropriate them."

Nov. 18

Make every effort to add to your faith, goodness; and to goodness, knowledge; and to knowledge, self-control; and to self-control, perseverance; and to perseverance, godliness; and to godliness, brotherly kindness; and to brotherly kindness, love.

[2 PETER 1:5-7]

"Tough assignment, yes, but with Me, all things are possible when you rely on My Strength, My Guidance, My Counsel, My Wisdom, My Love. Lean on Me. Trust Me. Follow Me. Walk beside Me. Do not stray, or tarry — lifeless and torn. Stay close beside Me, sheltered from the storm — strengthened within the storm. Fight the good fight from glory to glory. . . . faith →goodness →knowledge →self-control →perseverance →godliness →brotherly kindness →love. ~~ If you possess these qualities in increasing measure, you are protected from being ineffective. The greatest of these is love — love, balanced with self-control, and kept strong with perseverance."

Spirit Calling

Nov. 19

Many are the plans in a man's heart, but it is the LORD's Purpose that prevails.
[PROVERBS 19:21]

"The ways of man, the plans of man, are far less wise than Mine. Even the most well-meaning intentions can be redirected by My Spirit, if you have a humble, teachable heart. Your best effort may seem to you to have been thwarted by an unforeseen shift in direction. But watch and wait. You will see how that shift is My Guidance to accomplish My Work in a new and different way, for a new and different purpose. Trust Me. Be open; be led; be used; be fed. Take My Hand. Be at Peace. Be led into My new and Perfect Will."

Nov. 20

Where your treasure is, there your heart will be also.
[MATTHEW 6:21]

"Your treasures are vast. — But, Oh, some of them are good, and pure, and holy. . . . But, Oh, some are not. . . .— making your heart torn between two masters. So choose this day whom you shall serve."

Nov. 21

I baptize you with water for repentance. But after me will come One Who is more Powerful than I . . . He will baptize you with the Holy Spirit and with Fire.
[MATTHEW 3:11]

"I come with Power to set you on fire for Me, to do My Work in the hearts and minds and lives of those I love. I so love the world that I gave. So shall you give — give of yourself, your time, your resources — to further My Kingdom on earth, as it is in Heaven. I baptize you with My Spirit — immersing you in My Power — enabling you to feed and comfort and love the hurting, the mourning, the fearful, the lonely, the lost. I set you on fire. Do nothing in your own strength. Rely solely on My Power, My Love, My Spirit. Go forth in Peace, strengthened with My Power and My Love, led by the prompting of My Spirit."

Nov. 22

I delight greatly in the LORD; my soul rejoices in my God.
[ISAIAH 61:10a]

Let them praise His Name with dancing.
[PSALM 149:3a]

"Your thanks and praise and sheer delight in Me bring Joy to My Heart. If you only knew how I dance over you with Joy, you would want to be in constant communion with Me. That same Joy then would fill you to overflow in pure delight. Those who see My Face and hear My WORDS stand in awe — lifting their hands to Me — then drop to their knees and bow at My Feet. But as praise flows from their hearts, Joy floods their inner-most being, making them jump to their feet to dance before My throne. Dance, child, dance over Me with singing. Lift your hands in honor of Me. Rejoice!"

Nov. 23

Godliness with contentment is great gain.
[1 TIMOTHY 6:6]

"Contentment comes from total trust in Me. Trust! Praise! — the two weapons certain to send the spirit of discontentment fleeing, and fill you with Joy — unexplainable Joy in the midst of difficult times. Think how the prison doors were opened for Paul when he praised Me in songs. . . . So too, will I set you free from your prisons — prisons of fear, anger, distress, discontentment, apathy, depression . . . as you trust Me, and praise Me with songs of deliverance."

Nov. 24

Cease striving and know that I am God.
[PSALM 46:10a (NAS)]

When you pass through the waters, I will be with you. . . . When you walk through the fire, you will not be burned; the flames will not set you ablaze.
Do not be afraid for I am with you.
[ISAIAH 43:2,5a]

"My urgent message to you now is this. . . . Cease striving to be perfect in the world's eyes. Stop the haste, and rest at My Feet. Even in the midst of trouble and haste, stop your heart, stop your soul, stop your self and come to Me for rest in your spirit — your innermost being. Sense My nearness. Turn it into a moment of thanks and praise. Then lifted on wings like eagles, you can soar through your day, unhindered by stressful thoughts and haste. Calm within you, calms the storm around you. Be at rest. All is well — if all is well with your soul. So rest. Be at peace. Then go forth unafraid. I am with you to strengthen you and guide you. Take My Hand. Walk on. I am with you for the journey on."

Nov. 25

*We know that our old self was
crucified with Him.*
[ROMANS 6:6a]

"Why are you downcast? Are you feeling remorse? Are you feeling worthless over failures? A humble and contrite heart is what I desire of you. But when you have come to Me, remorseful and humble, and you ask for My help and My forgiveness, go on from here, rejoicing in My Love, My Mercy, My Grace and Forgiveness. Condemnation comes not from Me. You are My treasured possession. I know you will fail again, but My Love is unconditional. I love you, knowing your heart's desire is to please Me, to honor Me, to love Me — but your **self** gets in the way. Die to **self**, over and over, until one day you see your **self** on the cross. Then, it is finished."

Nov. 26

It is for freedom that Christ has set us free.
Stand firm, then, and do not let yourselves
be burdened again by a yoke of slavery.
[GALATIANS 5:1-3]

"My children need love the most when they are most unlovable. I came to set the captives free. It is for freedom that I came to set you free . . . free from pain . . . free from brokenness . . . free from fear . . . free from addictions, from lust, from pride — from all that separates you from Me. Tell, Me, child, tell Me. — What is it that is causing that chasm today? Repent of it now. . . . Then walk in freedom. For it is for freedom, I have come to set you free."

Nov. 27

How priceless is Your unfailing Love.
[PSALM 36:7a]

"Child, you honor Me, and bring Me Joy, when you praise Me for My Love and My Goodness and My Keeping Power — for My Provision, for My Presence — and when you take delight in My WORD — and when you want My Will to be done in your life. Live, act, move, love — according to My Will for you — and you will be filled with Peace and Joy, as you bring Me Joy and Honor in so doing."

Nov. 28

I have loved you with an Everlasting Love;
I have drawn you with Loving-Kindness.
[JEREMIAH 31:3]

"When you turned your life over to Me, I filled you to over-flowing with My Love — My Abundant Love. Rest in My Arms, until you feel My Love flow through you, healing all your inner hurts, struggles, and pain — cleansing you with My Pure Love. I anoint you with the Oil of Gladness instead of mourning. Come, child, let Me hide you in My Holiness and heal your broken heart. Know that I am here — ever beckoning you into My Presence. . . . So come."

Nov. 29

I praise You, Father, LORD of Heaven and Earth, because You have hidden these things from the wise and learned, and revealed them to little children. Yes, Father, for this was Your good pleasure.
[LUKE 10:21]

"I am anxious to share My Treasures with you. But first must come some training — training for you to learn to walk in the ways of the Father, and not in the ways of this dark world — plucking you out of the darkness, to walk in the Light of My Kingdom. I choose to reveal My Secrets to you when you rest in the Shadow of the Almighty, and when you choose Me over the evil desires of this age. So, choose life, and look for My Treasures stored up for you this side of heaven. Wait, watch, listen. In due time, I will reveal My Secret Treasures to your tender, childlike heart. First the training — then the treasures. Wait and watch, and you shall see them revealed to you in deeper and more wonderful ways."

Nov. 30

*Shouts of joy and victory resound in the
tents of the righteous.
"The LORD's Right Hand has
done mighty things!"*
[PSALM 118:15]

"Look ahead, only to anticipate the joy that awaits you. Look back, only at the TOWERS — the victories, the gladness, the love and training and blessings — and you will be filled with unspeakable joy and praise! Even in the midst of current sufferings, TOWERS from your past cause joy to ripple through your very being. Revisit those TOWERS."

Dec. 1

With God we will gain the victory.
[PSALM 108:13a]

"It may be a gray day outside, but you are reflecting My Light to the world around you, as you walk in the Light of My Victory. You are Mine. No foe can defeat you. Believe that. Live like you believe it. Cast out fear at every turn when the enemy rages. The battle is Mine, not yours. Pray and sing in the Spirit, and you will quickly be at peace. It sets the victory in motion. My Forces always win — making you the victor!"

Dec. 2

I have set the LORD always before me.
Because He is at my right hand,
I will not be shaken.
[PSALM 16:8]

"I will lead you and guide you when you put your hand in Mine. My Hand is ever reaching out to you. Catch hold of it, and I will take you to High Places you have yet to know. Reach out your hand to Mine, and I will touch you with My ever-available Love, My Power, My Spirit, My Life. Reach out to Me and I will guide you into all Truth — Truths you have yet to discover. So come, reach out and be held in My ever-keeping Power — My ever-available Love. Be held. Be loved. Be empowered. Be led."

Dec. 3

You have made known to me the path of life;
You will fill me with joy in Your Presence,
with eternal pleasures at Your Right Hand.
[PSALM 16:11]

"How often My children miss out on Blessings, and Favor, Mercy, Grace, Peace, Joy, Strength, and Provisions. Seeking My Presence is the prelude for receiving such as these. So much crowds Me out of your days, your life. Seek Me first — seek not answers to prayers — seek Me, My Presence, My Face, My Strong Loving Arms, holding you close. Then whisper your prayers to Me — your longings — your needs — your fears — your heart-cries for those you love. Listen for My Whispers in return. Such intimacy with Me is what is needed for the Life and Strength and godliness My seekers desire. Come into My Presence. Drink deeply from the Streams of Living Water flowing from My Presence. My Love is wooing you. Come."

Dec. 4

My eyes are fixed on You, O Sovereign LORD.
[PSALM 141:8a]

"Keep your eyes fixed on Me. As you love and worship Me, our eyes will meet and you will see the true beauty of My Kingdom. The Eyes of My Heart are always fixed on you. And when you come to Me and fix your eyes on Me, you find complete rest and peace and strength and Power — My Power — My Keeping Power flowing through you to live and to work according to My Spirit. Be still and be held in My Keeping Power."

Dec. 5

The WORD of God is living and active.
Sharper than any double-edged sword, it
penetrates even to dividing soul
and spirit, joints and marrow; it judges the
thoughts and attitudes of the heart.
[HEBREWS 4:12]

In the beginning was the WORD, and the
WORD was with God, and the WORD was God.
He was with God in
the beginning.
The WORD became flesh and made His
dwelling among us. We have seen His Glory.
[JOHN 1:1,2,14]

"My followers, and those who My followers reach out to, are often confused by the Triune God — the One True God — yet God Who is 3-in-1. This then, is the secret to that mystery. . . . God the Father spoke the WORD, and the world was created. — God the Father's WORD set the world in motion. I am that WORD. I set the world in motion. I set you in motion. I am the WORD made flesh. And now that I have returned to the Father, My Spirit is the Father's WORD living and active in you now. The WORD of God will never pass away. It is living and active in His followers. Listen for My Still, Small Voice revealing God's Powerful WORD."

Dec. 6

Delight yourself in the LORD and He will give you the desires of your heart.
[PSALM 37:4]

"Lean on Me. Continue to lean on Me, and I will give you the desires of your heart because those desires will become My desires for you. So lean — lean only on Me. Walk by My Side and you will be set free from stress and fears. Lean on Me, and wait in My Presence for My Touch. Then go forth in My Power — unafraid, unencumbered by the weight of sin."

Dec. 7

Be still and know that I am God.
[PSALM 46:10a]

How priceless is Your Unfailing Love!
[PSALM 36:7a]

He put a new song in my mouth, a hymn of praise to our God.
[PSALM 40:3a]

"Listen, child, and you shall hear the Voice from heaven saying, 'Be still and know that I am God.' Rest in My Arms of Love until you feel the pulse of My Spirit flow through your very being ~~ refreshing your soul as never before ~~ each time sweeter and more precious than the last. That is the secret of Kingdom living. Return to Me. Be refreshed. Go out singing, 'How priceless is Your Unfailing Love!'"

Dec. 8

There is now no condemnation for those who are in Christ Jesus.
[ROMANS 8:1]

"There is now no condemnation for you, since you are now in Me. Be aware that any condemnation you hear whispered to you, comes ONLY from the enemy. Correction and guidance come from your Loving Abba Father. Think how different is your soul, when you see and understand that one Truth. My Blood covers your sin, your mistakes, your failures. And now My Loving Care corrects and repairs and encourages and instructs; and leads and guides you along the correct path."

Dec. 9

My soul thirsts for God, for the Living God.
When can I go and meet with God?
[PSALM 42:2]

"You live with Me. Yes, abide with Me, and all else will be given you — pressed down and overflowing from the abundance of My Life Flow. Your King, Your Master, your Lover, your Friend — abide with Me — live connected with Me; and watch My Life — My abundant Life — flow through you in many sundry ways, you yet have not seen. Be open, be filled. Be used. Wait in My Presence until that Life Flow is pulsing through you. . . . That is all you need. . . . Now go forth and bear much fruit — sweet fruit to nourish and feed those hungry souls around you. Go forth in My Name. Go forth."

Dec. 10

I have told you this so that My Joy may be in you and that your Joy may be complete.
[JOHN 15:11]

"When you come to Me I must have your total devotion, for Me to reveal hidden Truths to you. Your senses must be turned off, for your spirit to join with My Spirit — to hear Me whisper My Truths to you. Sit at My Feet, drink in My Spirit, that your Joy may be complete."

Dec. 11

All my longings lie open before You, O LORD;
my sighing is not hidden from You.
I wait for You, O LORD;
You will answer, O LORD my God.
[PSALM 38:9,15]

"Come now. Come sit in My Presence. Search deep within your heart — what is it that you long for? What is that deep longing in your soul? What is that deep need that keeps draining your spirit? I want to hold you close. Lean in toward Me. Tell Me now. . . . What is it that is really gnawing at your inner-most being? I long to fill that need. . . . Tell Me now."

Dec. 12

My soul clings to You; Your Right Hand upholds me.
[PSALM 63:8]

"If I am really to be King of your heart, and Shepherd of your soul, and LORD of your self, you must bow your heart to My Will — not reluctantly — but rather, with immediate fervor. As you mature, this becomes more and more automatic, so that moment by moment, you bow to My Will. Learn to recognize My Voice among the clatter of the day. The deceiver will mimic Me, to lead you astray. Stand firm. He must then flee. Cling to Me, your King, your Shepherd, your Protector, your LORD. Cling to Me."

Dec. 13

Why are you so downcast, O my soul? Put your hope in God.
[PSALM 42:5,11; 43:5]

My heart says of You, "Seek His Face!" Your Face, LORD, I will seek.
[PSALM 27:8]

"Child, it is not I who condemns you; that is the workings of Satan and of your flesh. Yes, I convict you, but it is ever with Love, not chastening condemnation. I speak with a whisper, saying, 'Return to Me. Seek My Face and pursue it.' I want your love as much as you want Mine. No greater joy for Me than when one turns to Me out of Love and Joy. My Presence awaits you. My Love awaits you. Come, child, come. And be raptured up into My Loving Arms. No earthly woe can then tarry or torment you. Lean on Me — on My Loving Arms, and Joy will flood into your very heart. Experience My Touch, know Me, trust Me. I love you. Join Me in intimacy within My Courts. I love you. I bid you, 'Come.'"

Dec. 14

The LORD is my strength and my shield; my heart trusts in Him, and I am helped. My heart leaps for joy and I will give thanks to Him in song.
[Psalm 28:7]

"Your praises, your love, your thankful heart are priceless to My Heart. I created you to bring Me pleasure. You do bring Me pleasure when — out of your free will — you choose to praise Me out of a thankful loving heart. And as you emulate Me, you become a channel of My Agape Love — unconditional, selfless, forgiving, gracious, merciful, compassionate Love — bringing Joy and Peace and Strength to the lost, to the hurting, to the needy souls I bring into your life, into your path. There is no greater calling."

Dec. 15

Praise be to the Lord, to God our Savior, who daily bears our burdens.
[Psalm 68:19]

"Busyness is an enemy of My Kingdom. . . .
    —Too busy to listen
    —Too busy to sit in My Presence — even for 10 minutes
    —Too busy to pour out My Love onto others
    —Too busy
Drop your burdens at My Feet. Let Me shoulder those burdens. Take up My Yoke — instead of the yoke of bondage of this day's busyness — for My Yoke is light in comparison. Under My Yoke, you can prance through your day with deep-down joy, knowing that I am in control — in control of all you choose to give to Me."

Dec. 16

O LORD, be gracious to us, we long for You.
Be our strength every morning, our
salvation in
time of distress.
[ISAIAH 33:2]

"Seek Me first before the day crowds in on you. You are Mine — I am yours — draw into that oneness. Be refreshed by the Wind of My Spirit blowing away the chaff — displaying the full treasure of My Work in your life. You are set apart for Me — set apart for My Pleasures. Wherever I take you, you will be a sweet fragrance to those around you, after being filled with the essence of My Presence in Your life. You are Mine — set apart for Me. I will lead you on. Do not be afraid. Draw close to My Side. Dig deep into My WORD. There in, is your Surety, your Strength."

Dec. 17

Seek ye first the Kingdom of God, and His righteousness;
and all these things shall be added unto you.
[MATTHEW 6:33 (KJV)]

"Time spent with Me is not time lost, but time invested. The rest of your day will flow much smoother if you have invested in My Kingdom. The revenue reaped is far greater than what is sown."

Dec. 18

If from there you seek the LORD your God, you
will find Him if you look for Him with all
your heart and with
all your soul.
[Deuteronomy 4:29]

"Come away with Me into My Secret Place. Picture a little child running to its mother's arms of safety and love. Be that child. Come running into My Arms of Love, safe and secure, warmed and re-energized by My Love. I whisper gently, 'I love you, child. You are My treasured possession. Come away with Me.'"

Dec. 19

He has taken me to the banquet hall,
and His Banner over me is Love.
[SONG OF SONGS 2:4]

"My Love is a Protective Banner over you ~~ a healing balm to your soul ~~ healing your wounded spirit and broken heart. Lean on Me, and I will bring healing to your soul. My Love nurtures your spirit with Kindness, and Comfort beyond any human compassion. Seek union with Me, and there you will find an endless supply of My Unfailing Love."

Dec. 20

Finally, all of you, live in harmony with one another; be sympathetic, love as brothers, be compassionate and humble.
[1PETER 3:8]

"For compassion's sake, is the only reason to recall your hurts and pain. Past hurts and failures, and sins, give you empathy for the hurting, dying, and broken, in the world around you. But, child, let only My Spirit trigger those memories. If it is My Spirit, then you will know it, by its peaceful nature — not the hurting, stabbing pain that the enemy inflicts when he triggers those memories. Be watchful. Claim victory. Go forth in Peace, to show compassion to other hurting souls."

Dec. 21

Your Kingdom come, Your Will be done on earth as it is in heaven.
[MATTHEW 6:10]

"You have asked Me for special impartations of My Power. Get ready. It is coming. Be willing to walk with Me in it. Get ready! I have seated you with Me in the Heavenly Realm now. — Yes! Live in the Heavenly Realm now, rooted and grounded in faith — faith, that you will be used for My Glory — bringing the Heavenly Realm here into the earthly realm in which you live. Carry the Heavenly Realm with you wherever I take you. And in so doing, you will root and establish My Kingdom, and impart My Power onto all you touch. Walk with Me in the Heavenly Realm and do works even greater than I did. — You are My Arms and Hands, and My Touch of Power. Watch Me work in your life and in the lives of those around you. Remember, seated with Me in the Heavenly Realm, live and move in My Power."

Dec. 22

As a mother comforts her child,
so will I comfort you.
[ISAIAH 66:13a]

"Just know that whatever comes, you are not alone. You are being held close; as a mother nestles her baby, so I gather you into My Arms ~~ where you are safe. Fear not, for I am surely with you. Step-by-step along the weary way, be held, be comforted, be led. Trust in My Unfailing Love."

Dec. 23

I have loved you with an everlasting Love;
I have drawn you with Loving-Kindness.
[JEREMIAH 31:3]

"You are My child, My holy temple, My cherished warrior, My treasured child. I gather you into My Arms when you are watchful and ready. Let Me carry you through the day. You are My friend, My warrior, My companion — when you are willing and ready to walk with Me. Let go of all earthly things that hold you away from Me. Come with Me and I will give you rest. I will give you My Love, My Protection, My Care. Meet Me here. I love you, child."

Dec. 24

God is our refuge and strength, an ever-present help in trouble.
[PSALM 46:1]

"Even in the stormy days, I am speaking to you. Listen, child. In your inner being, I am there to calm your open heart. Yes, with an open heart and a listening ear of your spirit, you will hear My Spirit calling, "Peace! Be still!" Calm in the midst of the storm — that is My order for your day. Peace. Be still! I love you, child. That is enough for your heart to be at rest. Soak yourself in My Love whenever your spirit is at unrest. Quickly I am there. Rest in My Love."

Dec. 25

How awesome is the LORD Most High, the Great King over all the earth.

[PSALM 47:2]

He was despised and forsaken of men, a man of sorrows and acquainted with grief.

[ISAIAH 53:3]

"Out of My Great Love for you, I came to you as a babe wrapped in swaddling clothes — not as a King. I walked in human flesh to see life here through your eyes — to be acquainted with grief and your earthly sorrows.

Out of My Great Love for you, I came to show you the Way, the Truth, and the Life.

Out of My Great Love for you, I came as your Sacrificial Lamb — paying the ultimate Price for you.

Out of My Great Love for you, I come again as your Great King — gathering you — My Body — My Bride to Myself. . . .

Come now, to the manger and worship your King."

Dec. 26

We have different gifts, according to the grace given us. If a man's gift is prophesying, let him use it in proportion to his faith. If it is serving, let him serve; if it teaching, let him teach; if it is encouraging, let him encourage; if it is contributing to the needs of others, let him give generously; if it is leadership, let him govern diligently; if it is showing mercy, let him do it cheerfully.
[ROMANS 12:6-8]

"To each of My disciples, both past and present, I have given special gifts. To some, the gift of discernment; to some, the gift of prophesying; to some, the gift of teaching; to some, the gift of intercession; to some, the gift of love and mercy; to some, the gift of dreams and interpreting dreams; to some, the gift of serving; to some, the gift of encouragement; to some, the gift of leadership; to some, the gift of giving. Do not be afraid to use your gifts. My Spirit will lead you and guide you to use your gifts in the right way, at the right time, and to the right people — if you stay in a constant state of worship within your heart, constantly attuned to hear My Voice. Tune your ears to My Whispers. Fear not — despair not — that you are lacking gifts you witness others using. Trust your Creator — the God of all Wisdom and Strength. Stand in awe of Me."

Dec. 27

Blessed are those who hunger and thirst for righteousness for they will be filled.
[MATTHEW 5:6]

"You struggle with the flesh. You hunger for a deeper walk with Me. You seek a more intimate relationship with Me. But you see your failures and you fall into despair. Child, it blesses My Heart to see your true heart's desire is to love Me more, to spend more intimate time with Me in My Presence — in My Holy of Holies. And yet, you choose to spend your time on things that will pass away. Choose Life, child. I know in your heart you deeply desire that, but the flesh gets in the way. Speak to that old **self**, 'Old **self**, be gone!! You were crucified with Christ. And it is not you who lives in me, but the Spirit Who raised Christ Jesus from the dead. Old **self**, be gone!! — Never to rise again!' Then pray, 'Spirit of the Living God, come in Power, fall afresh on me.' Child, you hunger for Me — for a purer heart. I will pour My Kingdom Blessings down on you. Seek Me above all, and all these fruits of righteousness will be yours in increasing measure."

Dec. 28

Summon Your Power, O God; show us Your Strength, O God, as You have done before.
[PSALM 68:28]

"Listen, child, your mission is to pass along My Unfailing Love. My Strength will be here for you, for every task, every mission, I put you on. Always Patient — always Kind — always here for you. Always ready and willing to hear you. Call out to Me in everything — that you may have My Guidance, My Strength. Sit at My Feet and receive My Blessings, My Love, My Touch. Then go out, ever strengthened for the task at hand."

Dec. 29

Do everything in love.
[1 CORINTHIANS 16:14]

"Service given to Me is the KEY that unlocks the Joy and the Freedom in your soul. Seek to serve Me at every turn. Offer it up as a sacrifice of your heart, your spirit, your self. Serve as unto Me at every turn. Do everything in My Love . . . and it will change you."

Dec. 30

My Presence will go with you,
and I will give you rest.
[EXODUS 33:14]

"Long for Me. Rest in Me. Stop resisting the Arms that want to hold you and protect you from the evil pursuer. Bring Me your cares, your desires, your troubles, your heart. Think of Me, though, not just when you are overloaded with cares and needs — but each moment, know that I Am Ever-Present, Ever-Loving, Ever-Caring . . . ever longing to hold you near. Rest in My Arms, child. Rest and be at peace. Abide with Me in the Secret Place. Moment . . . by moment . . . abide. Keep an open ear, an open heart . . . abide."

Dec. 31

*L*ORD, *You establish peace for us;*
all that we have accomplished
You have done for us.
[ISAIAH 26:12]

"As a mother smiles and is warmed by her baby saying, 'I love you, Mommy,' so I am warmed by your delight in Me. Draw near to Me. Sense My Presence there with you now. I will reveal to you the plans I have in store for you, each step at a time. Put all thoughts of tomorrow away. Be still and know that I am your source of Life — your source of Strength and Joy and Peace — each day ahead. Focus each day on hearing My Guidance — on hearing how you can better serve Me, love Me, and devote your life to My Purposes for you. Stay close by My Side throughout each day. And I will be here for you at every turn. Go forth now in Joy, knowing I am here for you at every turn."

INDEX

Bride of Christ
Feb. 9
June 21
July 17

Burdens
Feb. 5
March 4
April 22
Aug. 22
Sept. 10
Dec. 15

Busyness
Dec. 15

Cease striving
Nov. 24

Child of God
Jan. 25
Feb. 3
Feb. 23
March 7
March 28
April 4
April 24
May 27
Nov. 15
Nov. 29
Dec. 18
Dec. 23

Choose this day
July 23
Nov. 20

Come to Me
Jan. 20
Jan. 22
Feb. 11
Feb. 12
Feb. 16
Feb. 17
Feb. 19
March 28
April 4
April 19
April 28
May 11
May 28
June 2
June 22
June 26
July 1
Aug. 13
Aug. 15
Aug. 21
Sept. 4
Sept. 27
Oct. 27
Nov. 11
Nov. 28
Dec. 3
Dec. 13

Comfort
Jan. 8
Jan. 30
Feb. 3
April 16
May 25

June 24
Aug. 17
Oct. 16
Dec. 19
Dec. 22

Companion
Jan. 8
Feb. 11
March 11
March 26
June 9
July 28
Aug. 8
Aug. 20
Aug. 21
Aug. 26
Sept. 9
Sept. 11

Compassion
April 16
April 22
April 25
Aug. 29
Sept. 26
Oct. 16
Oct. 27
Nov. 3
Dec. 19
Dec. 20

Completion
Sept. 8

Condemnation
Jan. 12
Sept. 6
Sept. 22
Dec. 8
Dec. 13

Confession
June 7
July 22
Aug. 22
Sept. 30

Contentment
Nov. 23

Creation
March 1
June 1
July 7
Oct. 8

Dance
Nov. 22

Darkness
March 22
July 3
July 22
Oct. 2
Oct. 3
Oct. 13
Nov. 3
Nov. 29

<u>Desires</u>
Jan. 31
April 18
Nov. 14
Dec. 6
Dec. 11

<u>Devotion</u>
March 15
May 30
Sept. 18
Oct. 22
Oct. 23
Oct. 30

<u>Disciple</u>
Feb. 7
May 30
July 16

<u>Discipline</u>
Jan. 5
Jan. 9
Jan. 24
Jan. 26
Feb. 15
May 8
May 30
July 19
July 23
Sept. 10
Sept. 20
Oct. 1
Oct. 3
Oct. 5

Oct. 17
Nov. 18
Nov. 29

<u>Do everything in love</u>
Sept. 26

<u>Do not ignore Me</u>
July 10
Aug. 5

<u>Equipped</u>
June 25
July 19

<u>Embrace</u>
Jan. 9
Jan. 22
March 8
April 6
April 20
May 11
June 11
June 15
June 28
July 1
July 9
July 13
Sept. 4
Sept. 27

<u>Encouragement</u>
Jan. 3
Jan. 6
Jan. 8

Jan. 12
Jan. 22
Jan. 30
Feb. 6
Feb. 12
Feb. 13
Feb. 15
Feb. 22
Feb. 25
March 4
March 5
March 10
March 16
March 20
March 21
March 30
April 1
April 3
April 6
April 9
April 15
April 17
April 19
April 22
May 2
May 25
May 28
May 29
June 9
June 10
June 12-15
June 22
June 25
July 9
July 19

July 24
July 30
Aug. 12
Aug. 22
Sept. 15
Sept. 16
Sept. 22-24
Oct. 7
Oct. 9-11
Oct. 25
Oct. 27-29
Nov. 5
Nov. 7
Nov. 27
Dec. 4
Dec. 13
Dec. 14
Dec. 19
Dec. 22-24
Dec. 27
Dec. 28
Dec. 31

Fast
Nov. 14

Fear
Jan. 30
Feb. 10
March 23
April 8
April 20
May 9
May 23
May 28

July 26
Oct. 18
Nov. 10

Fix your eyes
March 10
April 3
July 30
Sept. 3
Sept. 19
Oct. 20
Oct. 23
Dec. 4

Fix your thoughts
Jan. 10
March 10
April 3
July 12
July 30
Aug. 6
Sept. 3
Sept. 14
Sept. 19
Oct. 20
Oct. 23

Flesh
Jan. 31
June 12
Dec. 13
Dec. 27

Flower
Sept. 15

Forgiveness
Jan. 12
Jan. 29
May 10
July 20
July 22
Aug. 22
Sept. 6
Sept. 30
Oct. 2
Nov. 25

Free/Freedom
Feb. 1
Feb. 2
Feb. 12
Feb. 20-22
Feb. 26
March 9
March 26
March 27
April 21
May 10
June 4
July 4
July 20
July 22
July 31
Aug. 1
Aug. 21
Aug. 26
Sept. 30
Oct. 18
Nov. 23
Nov. 26

Friend
Jan. 17
March 10
March 11
March 25
May 5
May 29
June 9
June 14
July 9
July 28
Aug. 11
Aug. 20
Aug. 21
Sept. 24
Sept. 29
Nov. 7

Fruit
Feb. 7
May 2
May 16

Garden
May 1
June 1

Gifts of the Spirit
Jan. 19
Jan. 21
April 5
Dec. 26

Give
Oct. 14

Nov. 12

Good things
March 16
Oct. 9
Nov. 16

Great King
Dec. 25

Guidance
Jan. 7
Jan. 18
Feb. 18
Feb. 21
Feb. 22
March 16
March 19
April 13
April 15
May 7
Aug. 9
Aug. 19
Oct. 7
Nov. 19
Dec. 31

Healing
Jan. 13
March 6
March 18
April 16
April 23
May 25
June 24
Dec. 19

Healing Balm
June 24
Dec. 19

Heavenly Realm
Dec. 21
Held
April 15
June 19
June 24
July 28
Dec. 2
Dec. 4
Dec. 22

Holy
April 11
May 8

Holy of Holies
Jan. 6
Jan. 17
March 6
March 15
May 27
Sept. 27

Holy Spirit
Jan. 1
Feb. 2
Feb. 9
April 23
June 21
June 27
June 29

Oct. 21
Nov. 2
Nov. 21
Dec. 7

Honor your parents
July 11

Hope
June 14
July 2
July 25
Sept. 24
Oct. 4

Humble
Jan. 26
Feb. 23
March 6
March 12
March 29
April 1
April 27
May 3
Aug. 30

Hurting
Jan. 21
Feb. 14
Aug. 2
Aug. 17
Nov. 15
Dec. 20

I AM
Jan. 8

June 9
Aug. 24
Sept. 16
Oct. 30

<u>Intimacy with Me</u>
Jan. 3
Jan. 10
Jan. 22
Feb. 11
Feb. 17-19
March 3
March 8
March 10-15
March 21
March 25
April 2
April 4
April 10
April 11
April 21
April 28
May 1
May 5
May 15
May 18
May 24
June 5
June 6
June 11
June 15
June 22
June 26-28
June 30
July 1

July 28
July 30
Aug. 1
Aug. 3
Aug. 16
Aug. 20
Aug. 21
Aug. 25
Aug. 26
Sept. 8
Sept. 9
Sept. 11
Sept. 18
Sept. 27
Oct. 11
Oct. 28
Nov. 2
Nov. 7
Nov. 11
Dec. 3
Dec. 4
Dec. 7
Dec. 11
Dec. 13
Dec. 16

<u>Invested</u>
Dec. 17

<u>It is finished</u>
Nov. 25

<u>Joy</u>
Feb. 2
Feb. 27

June 14
June 22
Sept. 18
Sept. 19
Sept. 24
Oct. 26
Nov. 5
Nov. 22
Nov. 23
Nov. 27
Nov. 30
Dec. 10

<u>Kingdom Living</u>
Jan. 17
Jan. 24
Feb. 17
Feb. 23
March 17
April 4
April 7
April 12
April 24
April 26
May 6
May 17
May 22
May 23
May 27
July 17
July 21
Aug. 8
Aug. 25
Sept. 20
Sept. 29

Oct. 2
Oct. 19
Nov. 12
Nov. 21
Dec. 7
Dec. 21

<u>Know Me</u>
Feb. 19
April 2
May 5
May 23
June 11
June 30
July 6
July 8
July 14

<u>Lean on Me</u>
Jan. 13
Feb. 3
Feb. 27
March 4
March 19
March 30
April 9
April 15
May 13
Sept. 13
Nov. 18
Dec. 6
Dec. 13
Dec. 19

<u>"Let there be. . ."</u>

Sept. 11
Sept. 18
Sept. 26
Oct. 5
Oct. 14
Oct. 19
Oct. 24
Oct. 27
Oct. 28
Nov. 4
Nov. 7
Nov. 15
Nov. 27
Nov. 28
Dec. 7
Dec. 13
Dec. 14
Dec. 19
Dec. 23
Dec. 25
Dec. 29

<u>Majesty</u>
March 1
March 17
May 24
June 1
July 7
July 8
Sept. 20

<u>Mind of Christ</u>
March 7
Sept. 14

<u>Mine</u>
Feb. 17

<u>Ministry/Service</u>
Jan. 1
Jan. 11
Jan. 16
Jan. 19
Jan. 21
Jan. 28
Feb. 6
Feb. 8
Feb. 21
Feb. 28
March 9
March 13
March 17
March 19
March 20
April 5
April 16
April 25
May 3
May 9
May 19
May 23
June 18
June 25
July 13
July 19
July 21
Aug. 2
Sept. 14
Sept. 17
Sept. 26

Feb. 22
Feb. 24
March 2
July 3
Aug. 11
Aug. 22
Nov. 7
Dec. 24
Dec. 31

<u>Persevere</u>
May 13
Sept. 24
Nov. 18

<u>Potter</u>
Jan. 5
June 19

<u>Power</u>
Jan. 28
Feb. 29
March 12
March 17
March 18
March 24
March 27
April 4
April 12
April 16
April 18
April 23
May 20
May 23
June 17

June 21
June 27
June 29
July 3
Sept. 13
Sept. 25
Sept. 28
Oct. 6
Oct. 9
Oct. 12
Oct. 21
Nov. 6
Nov. 9
Nov. 21
Dec. 4
Dec. 21

<u>Prayer</u>
March 29
May 20
June 7
July 9
Oct. 6

<u>Presence</u>
Jan. 6
Jan. 22
Feb. 2
Feb. 8
March 3
March 8
March 15
March 25
April 28
May 11

Feb. 16
Feb. 19
Feb. 24
Feb. 28
April 3
April 9
April 10
April 13
April 19
July 29
Aug. 4
Aug. 13
Aug. 22
Nov. 24
Dec. 24
Dec. 30

<u>Return to Me</u>
June 2
Nov. 14
Dec. 13

<u>Reward</u>
Jan. 17
July 24
Sept. 29

<u>Run the Race</u>
May 8

<u>Saved</u>
Feb. 20
Sept. 1

<u>Secret Place</u>
Jan. 18

March 24
May 15
June 6
July 13
Aug. 4
Oct. 11
Nov. 7
Dec. 18
Dec. 30

<u>Seek Me</u>
Jan. 10
Jan. 17
Jan. 18
Jan. 23
April 3
April 10
May 17
May 28
May 29
June 3
June 20
June 26
June 27
June 30
July 3
July 6
July 27
Aug. 5
Aug. 14
Sept. 7
Sept. 20
Oct. 30
Dec. 16

<u>See Me at work</u>

Jan. 28
Feb. 9
March 1
March 9
March 18
April 12
May 12
May 23
May 31
June 29
July 2
July 6
July 7
July 16
Aug. 14
Sept. 25
Oct. 12
Oct. 16
Nov. 17
Dec. 21

Self
Jan. 15
Jan. 31
Feb. 1
Feb. 21
March 12
March 24
March 26
April 30
May 21
May 26
Sept. 2
Sept. 10
Sept. 12

Oct. 1
Oct. 6
Oct. 31
Nov. 25
Dec. 27

Set apart
March 19
Sept. 19
Oct. 23
Oct. 30
Dec. 16

Sheep
May 7
Aug. 9

Sorrow
Feb. 3
June 24
Dec. 25

Stand Firm
March 22

Strength
Jan. 8
March 24
July 3
Sept. 13
Nov. 17
Dec. 28
Dec. 31

Suffering
Jan. 8

June 14
July 24
Sept. 24
Oct. 4
Oct. 16

Surrender
Jan. 5
March 11
March 15
April 7
April 29
April 30
May 7
May 21
June 12
June 19
June 29
July 10
July 23
Aug. 10
Sept. 17
Oct. 1
Oct. 22
Dec. 12

Taken away
Nov. 13

Tapestry
Aug. 17

Tongue
Feb. 4
April 18
July 5

Towers
Nov. 30

Transformed
March 25
April 11
May 3
May 5
June 15
June 19
June 26
Aug. 3
Sept. 8
Sept. 12
Nov. 18

Treasures
March 28
April 4
Aug. 8
Aug. 28
Oct. 26
Nov. 13
Nov. 20
Nov. 29

Triune God
July 8
Dec. 5

Trouble
Jan. 20
March 5
May 20

July 24
Oct. 10
Nov. 24
Dec. 24

Trust
Jan. 14
Jan. 30
Feb. 19
March 16
April 6
April 8
April 15
April 20
April 22
April 25
April 27
May 2
May 22
May 30
July 2
July 24
July 26
Aug. 7
Aug. 17
Aug. 31
Sept. 4
Oct. 15
Nov. 10
Nov. 19
Nov. 23

Victory
Feb. 10
March 17
June 16

June 17
June 29
Sept. 2
Sept. 28
Oct. 20
Nov. 6
Dec. 1

Wait
Jan. 14
May 31
July 2
Aug. 7
Aug. 27

Weakness
Jan. 4
March 5
April 16
April 27
May 3
Nov. 17

Weary
Jan. 20
Jan. 22
Feb. 3
April 9
May 13
May 28
Aug. 13

Well done
Feb. 6

Well with your soul

Dec. 23

Yearning after Me
Jan. 23
July 9

Yoke
Feb. 5
March 26
April 29
June 12
Sept. 7
Sept. 10
Dec. 15

You are Mine
Jan. 12
Feb. 3
Feb. 10
Feb. 12
Feb. 16
March 5
March 8
March 10
March 27
April 3
April 22
May 15
June 17
July 30
July 31
Aug. 12
Nov. 4
Nov. 5
Dec. 1
Dec. 16

CPSIA information can be obtained at www.ICGtesting.com
Printed in the USA
LVOW051537110613

338061LV00002B/176/P